Thematic Patterns of Emily Dickinson's Poetry

Neeru Tandon
Anjana Trivedi

ATLANTIC
PUBLISHERS & DISTRIBUTORS (P) LTD

Published by

ATLANTIC

PUBLISHERS & DISTRIBUTORS (P) LTD

B-2, Vishal Enclave, Opp. Rajouri Garden,
New Delhi-110027
Phones : +91-11-25413460, 25429987, 25466842

Sales Office
7/22, Ansari Road, Darya Ganj,
New Delhi-110002
Phones : +91-11-23273880, 23275880, 23280451
Fax : +91-11-23285873
web : www.atlanticbooks.com
e-mail : info@atlanticbooks.com

Chennai Branch
5, Nallathambi Street, Wallajah Road,
Chennai-600002
Phones : +91-44-64611085, 32413319
e-mail : chennai@atlanticbooks.com

ISBN 978-81-269-0929-2

Printed in India
at Nice Printing Press, Delhi

PREFACE

> "Poetry seems to flow out of her involuntarily like a mountain rill."

This is absolutely true in case of Emily Dickinson. Her perception of beauty is so keen that she sees it even in a locomotive. Themes and imagery of her poems are borrowed from ordinary life and the things around her. A poet of romantic sensibility, Dickinson's sensitive soul throbbed to the song of the oriole, to the ray of light in winter and to the thousand little things that made her world glow with beauty. With a great spirit of religious unorthodoxy Dickinson relies more on her soul to lead her to Heaven and to God than all the sermons and church-goings that conventional religion recommends. In fact she discarded the sway of reason and relied more on intuition and imagination. In "Pappa Above" Emily mocks the anthropomorphic concept of God. In her poems she refers to Him as 'a noted clergyman' and flippantly salutes Him as 'Burglar', 'Banker, Father!' But in spite of her scornful attitude to the traditional picture of the Puritan's God, we find in her, true piety and a deep faith in Heaven and Immortality.

This young woman who shut herself up in a narrow world, found within her narrow world details that stirred her poetic soul to rapturous heights. The charm of her poetry lies in her unrivalled ability to convey varied states of mind through suggestive pictures. Abstractions lead themselves to pictorial treatment at the hands of this woman with genius.

If nature occupies a prominent place in the poetry of Emily Dickinson, there are other themes that the poetess continually gave expression to. These are the Soul, Life, and Immortality. The greatness of Emily Dickinson lies in the fact that to these ideas she gave concrete shape.

She is a major American poet, a recluse, nicknamed the 'Nun of Amherst'. Only seven of her 1800 poems were published during her lifetime, five of them in the *Springfield Republican*. Dickinson never married. She withdrew from social contact and devoted herself in secret into writing. She said:

"I felt a Cleaving in my Mind–
As if my Brain had split–
I tried to match it–Seam by seam–
But could not make them fit.
The thought behind, I strove to join
Unto the thought before–"

There are no titles given by Emily Dickinson to her poems. In the anthologies the arrangement is chronological, the index of first lines alone does not provide adequate means of recognition. The classification was based principally on key words in the poems themselves. In instances in which the whole content is stated in terms of imagery, the image itself, rather than the meaning, is used as a heading. Certain large groups, such as those headed LIFE, LOVE and DEATH, contain the bulk of the poems. In some instances, however, a poem listed under one of these headings will have also an entry under one or more categories. For example, 'Death is a dialogue between/The Spirit and the Dust' is entered under Death, Spirit, and Dust by the editors. So mostly, what is important to categorise her poem is the poem number and the first line of the poem is given as the title of the poem in order to make it convenient for the readers and critics. We could not resist the urge to re-examine the poems of Emily Dickinson and to pursue and scrutinize her poetic works and letters, through a fresh magnifying glass of understanding and, if possible, to revalidate her thematic material. The book also gives a background of American Poetry and Emily Dickinson's place in it. Different chapters discuss the themes of her poems in complete detail. The style and technique used in her poetry is presented through a different angle. We hope it will serve the purpose of students and researchers of Emily Dickinson.

Neeru Tandon
Anjana Trivedi

INTRODUCTION

American Poetry and Emily Dickinson

> "Poetry is as ancient as the human race. In all cultures of the world, the Mantras are in verse."

American literature had a long period of apprenticeship. It fumbled like all other literatures of the world. American literature begins with the first English colonies at Playmouth and Boston. The American people from colonial times until now have written countless essays and songs, poems and plays, novels and short stories. The growth of American literature is bound up with the growth of America as a nation.

Narrative poetry has been written from the days of the New Englanders to the present. It has not been of very high quality. Longfellow's and Whittier's stories in verse have a tempo that is exciting and stimulating. This same pace is found in such Modern Poetry as Edwin Arlington Robinson's *Tristram* and Stephen Vincent Benet's *John Brown's Body*. Lyrical poetry has been abundantly written. The musical, rippling verse of Sidney Lanier and the haunting magical lines of Edgar Allan Poe are pleasing to the ear when read aloud. The subtle and flexible rhythms of Emily Dickinson conceal flashes of beauty. Walt Whitman wrote free verse which had no rhyme or meter but had a marked rhythm and pulse within it.

In the nineteenth century, the three great poets were Ralph Waldo Emerson, Walt Whitman and Emily Dickinson. Whitman's poems represent his world and himself. In Randall Jarrell's *The New Pelican Guide to American Literature*, (ed.)

Boris Ford] observes: "Of all modern poets, he has, quantitatively speaking the most comprehensive soul and qualitatively a most comprehensive and comprehending one". He was a 'very American Poet'. He was the greatest of Bards because of the favouring circumstances of a democratic ideal and an open society. He was by birth and education a poet 'of the people' more than any previous American writer was. Whitman's poetry was poetry of sweet sensations, uninhibited imagination and a violent joy in life. He encompasses within the ambit of his poems, himself and every other American, his nation, love, death, pantheistic God in every object, the future and eternity as well.

As a poet, Emerson was a rebel. To Emerson, poetry was a function of his own being. "The poet is the student, the receiver of wisdom, not the teacher. Poetry is moral, but it is not didactic".*

Emily Dickinson was one of the great poets of all time, perhaps, the greatest of all American women poets. Her body of poems is a religious quest. Her universe was that of the soul; her special task was to render that universe a living spirit. She faced a problem to find her own integrity and her own unique mode of expression. She wrote of God, Man and Nature and knew love and death intimately as few ever did.

On April 15, 1862, when Thomas Wentworth Higginson (1823-1911), a writer and reformer, received a letter from Emily Dickinson enclosing four of her poems, it became a significant date in the history of American poetry. She, then thirty-one years old, was writing to a professional man of letters to inquire whether her verses 'breathed'. She knew him to be a liberal thinker, interested in the status of women in general and women writers in particular. The importance of the correspondence with Higginson, thus initiated, and continued

* Spiller, R.E. *The Cycle of American Literature.*

throughout Emily Dickinson's life, and cannot be exaggerated. In the first place, the four poems she initially selected reveal that in 1862 the poet was no longer novice but an artist whose strikingly original talent was fully developed. She enclosed:

"Safe in their Alabaster Chambers" (216),
"I'll tell you how the Sun rose" (318),
"The nearest Dream recedes—unrealised" (319),
and "We play at paste" (320)

Higginson's problem was compounded by the fact that during Emily Dickinson's lifetime he was never convinced that she wrote poetry. The first weeks of their letter exchange were critical in Emily Dickinson's literary life. The second letter to Higginson, written ten days later, enclosed three poems: "South Winds jostle them" (86), "Of all the sounds dispatched abroad" (321) and "There came a day at Summen's full" (322). Like the previous four, they were selected for their range of themc and prosodic variety. The lapse of six weeks before she wrote again, in view of the nature of the third letter, suggests that between April 25 and June 7, she accepted her destiny as an artist who in her lifetime would remain unknown.

Thenceforth, she contented herself by enclosing or incorporating verses from time to time in letters to friends. The number thus communicated was but a minuscule fraction of what she was writing, and since the selections were made for particular occasions, they seldom reveal the intellectual and emotional depths she could plumb. Her growing preoccupation with the subject of fame is a striking characteristic of the poems written between 1862 and 1865.

Thereafter, throughout her life, Emily Dickinson continued to write poetry, but never again with the urgency she experienced in the early 1860's, when she fully developed her 'flood subjects' on the themes of living and dying. With paradoxes of extraordinary insight she repeatedly gives relationship to the ideas and experience which exist in time but never are a part of it.

The publication of *Poems by Emily Dickinson* by Roberts Brothers of Boston nevertheless proved to be one of the literary events of 1890, and the reception of the slender volume encouraged the editors to select 166 more verses, issued a year later as *Poems, Second Series*. These, likewise, were warmly received. In 1896 Mrs. Todd alone edited *Poems, Third Series*, bringing the total number published to 449, and together with 102 additional poems and parts of poems included in Mrs. Todd's edition of *Letters of Emily Dickinson* (1894), they constituted the Dickinson canon until 1914, when Emily Dickinson's niece and literary heir, Martha Dickinson Bianchi, issued *The Single Hound*.

By now the public had come to appreciate the quality of Dickinson's originalities, and alterations in the text of *The Single Hound* are refreshingly few. But Mrs. Bianchi sometimes had trouble reading the manuscripts, and on occasion, words or phrases were misread, in that volume and in the two later ones, which completed publication of all the verses in Mrs. Bianchi's possession, *Further Poems* (1929) and *Unpublished Poems* (1935). The appearance of *Both of Melody* (1945) from texts prepared by Mrs. Todd and her daughter, Millicent Todd Bingham, virtually completed publication of all the Dickinson poetry, and marked a new era in textual fidelity. It presented 668 poems and fragments deriving from transcripts made by Mrs. Todd, or from manuscripts which had remained among her papers.

CONTENTS

EMILY DICKINSON: AN INTRODUCTION

1

About the year, 1930, a scion of a Puritan family in England crossed the Atlantic ocean with his small family and settled down in the Connecticut Vallery to carve out his career in the new world. The reason for this migration seems to have been the unpropitious political climate for the Presbytarian Church. The first ancestor settling in this part of New England was thus the pilgrim father to the Dickinson family of Amherst which sprang into prominence through the dedicated religious and educational activities of Samuel Fowller Dickinson, Emily's grandfather.

Emily Dickinson's grandfather; a lawyer by profession, devoted himself to the advancement of Christianity and bequeathed to his family the responsibilities of that cause. His son, Edmund Dickinson, inherited his father's practice along with the obligations to church and college. By the time, Emily Dickinson was born in this family, the Puritan Theocracy had made its last stand. It was no longer able to democratc New England. Its foundations were tottering. Yet Amherst in 1830, was still a Puritan village with its life centred in the church and college, controlled by the church.

Emily Dickinson was born on December 10, 1830, in Amherst Massachussett. Amherst was a small town, but was quiet thickly-wooded area of the Connecticut Metropoles. It was equity rules away from Boston and Cambridge. Her father was the treasurer of the college and leading citizen of the town.

She was probably guilty of her slight figure, was reticent and avoided photographers. Some biographers attribute this indifference to her lack of good features. She lived the life of a recluse, perfectly devoid of outward event, remained unknown during her life time and died in the same little town of Amherst where her grandfather had been a leader in founding Amherst college. Her father, Edmund Dickinson, educated at Yale, followed the family profession of law and became member of congress and served the college in the capacity of a treasurer for nearly forty years. It was his custom, once a year, to hold a large reception at his house, attended by all the families connected with the institution and by the leading people of the town. On these occasions, his daughter, Emily emerged from her wonted retirement and did her part as a gracious hostess. The annual occasion once past, she withdrew again into her seclusion. Except for three intervals of a few months each, she lived constantly at home. Her father, who dominated the house-hold with kindly austerity, liked to have his family about him. He persuaded his sons to become his successor and next-door neighbour. Neither of his daughters married. The fact that her family circle remained unbroken until her father's death in 1874, made it possible for Emily Dickinson to maintain her childhood relation to her parents almost to the end of her own life. To those of her blood, she was attached with a consuming loyalty.

To Emily Dickinson, her father was a cardinal fact only where he is taken for granted. Without him her personality cannot be properly interpreted. His gods were her gods. His granite integrity was hers also. As a child she stood in no little awe of him and there were moments in her later girlhood when flesh and blood threatened to mutiny. But defiance of her father was the defiance of what was deepest in herself, an instinct of rightness that could not be denied.

Emily Dickinson came to understand and respect her father as her own soul. She had known other brilliant and prominent men but none to match her father. She wrote after his death that his heart was pure and terrible and perhaps no other like it existed. Her father was a stern moralist, reserved in manners and had a marked individuality in thought and love of independence: "When he spoke, his timid wife trembled, obeyed and was silent."[1]

Emily Dickinson herself exclaimed for the strict conservative nature of her father : "If father is asleep on the lounge, the house is full."[2] Thus her father dominated the household and her gentle and colourless mother lived in his shadow. Her mother was the type of gentle submissive woman that stirs the possessive and protective instinct of intensely masculine men. Her name was also Emily and she was a cold, religious, hard-working housewife, who suffered from depression. She reverend her husband and devoted her life to making his home a silken nest. Higinson, a little stunned, recalled what Emily had said to him in summary way; "I never had a mother. I suppose a mother is one to whom you hurry when you are troubled."[3] Mrs. Dickinson was hardly qualified to a tower of strength but ten years after Higginson's visit. Emily would not have been able to dismiss their relationship so cavalierly. Just twelve months after her husband's death. Mrs. Dickinson became paralysed and lingered for seven years as an invalid. Her only companion was her fathers clerk, Benjamin Newton. This explains her sense of withdrawal and isolation in her life. She was terribly shaken after her father's death. In 1853, her only masculine contact, a friend and possible a guide, Benjamin died. These developments are highlighted by her biographers.

Dickinson thus exhibits mixed elements as a poet of 19th Century America. That is why she is bracketed with Poe and Whitman as an exponent of all that 19th Century America symbolised. She never wrote them with an eye on seeing them in print or make money or reputation.

Since Emily Dickinson left contacts with the outside world, large part of the care of her mother must have fallen to her share. Her mother had become her child. Before Mrs. Dickinson died on November 14, 1882, Emily had learned that she had a monther.

Emily Dickinson's brother, William Austin Dickinson, was closely patterned after the parental model. His local attachments grew into the most consuming interests in his life. He became intensely parochial, hating to lcavc thc town even for a pleasure trip. When, he died on August 16, 1895, town, church, college, paid fitting honour to the memory of a beloved and faithful citizen. As a young man he had wished to establish himself in a flourishing western city to grow up with the country, but he was ever persuaded by his father to remain at home. His marriage (July 1856) brought into the closely knit Dickinson family an alien and dazzling personality, Susan Gilbert, a former school mate of Emily's at Amherst Academy. Emily accepted her with overflowing enthusiasm. Emily was much in brother's house and Susan in hers. Messages flew between them. Thus, her sister-in law, Susan Gilbert, a worldly "New Yorker", became Emily's confidante and she became the most comprehending and mentally stimulating influence in Emily's life. But gradually they drifted further and farther apart. The only link between the two divided households was Austin's second son Gilbert but when the entrancing child died in 1883, the link was broken.

Emily always dressed in white, was always a model of the affectionate aunt, helping to solve their dilemmas with sympathetic comprehension, delighting in their saying, watching their games with amused interest.

Emily's sister, Lavinia, was a lifelong companion and trusted confidante. Her attachment with Lavinia was earnest and indissoluble. Without her, life was fear and paradise a cowardice except for her inciting voice. It was to her sister only that Emily spoke of the man who was closest to her heart.

Apparently without any such psychic crisis as Emily under went, she remained at home and quietly accepted her destiny as high priestess of Dickinson's household. Whatever her father, brother, or sister said or did or thought, was right in her eyes. No other view was possible.

Thus Lavinia held the world at bay, while Emily confronted eternity. Ultimately it was owing to Lavinia's childlike faith in the supreme importance of anything her adored sister had written that Emily's letter to the world was not irrecoverably lost. Before she died in August 31, 1897, Lavinia knew that Emily's triumph was secure.

Thus seven generations of Dickinson, uncompromisingly going their own way, and thinking their own thoughts, had built up the rich soil of Emily's inheritance and formed the most important influence on shaping her character.

Before her eleventh birthday, Emily had begun to attend Amherst Academy. At that time it was a flourishing New England School, conducted by a principal, with one or more male assistants and preceptress was especially charged with the education of girls. Unconsciously Emily was building up in childhood the store of little nameless but vividly remembered experiences that constitute the poet's stock in trade.

Though a good student, Emily dreaded examinations and exhibitions. She had no inclination to display her talents in public. In August 1845, she wrote to Abiah :

> I am already gasping in view of our examination and although I am determined not to dread it, I know it is so foolish, yet in spite of my heroic resolutions. I cannot avoid a few misgivings when I think of those tall, stern, trustees. ......[4]

Towards every other aspect of her school, however, Emily was eager and ever ecstatic. Her devotion to the youngmen and women who were her teachers knew no bounds. If she considered her school master's death her "first affliction", it was because she was sensitive to the grief of the village and was willing to make it her very own. In fact, Emily's relation to her admired young teacher was not closer than Milton's to Edward King. Her girlish letter shows her trying with all her might to weep for the local Iycidas - "the departed Humphrey,".

When Emily Dickinson was sixteen, she realized her fondest hope. In the autumn of 1847, she was enrolled as one of the two hundred thirty five members of Mary Lyon's family at Mount Halyoke, the institution providing growth of mind and character. Emily liked her friends, class-mates, her work and her teachers. In this particular institution, girls were free to receive callers or to visit away on appropriate occasion. Religious activity reforming spiritual health was a major part of school life. She wrote to Abiah Root :

> I love the seminary and the teachers are bound strongly to my heart by ties of affection. I have

> neglected the one thing needful when all were obtaining it and I may never, never again pass through such a season as was granted us last winter.[5]

Her confidence continues :

> ... I regret the last term when that golden opportunity was mine, that I did not give up and become a Christian. It is now too late so my friends tell me, so my offended conscience whispers but it is hard for me to give up the world.[6]

Some change came over. The things which brought zest and zeal to her, declined to do so. The society of teachers and classmates, for which her enthusiasm had been unbounded in the winter, she was beginning to find tiresome. She wrote to Abiah :

> "Father had decided not send me to Holyoke another year, so this is my last term".[7] Her father must have taken up this decision for the sake of Emily's health. Moreover home was dear to her.

Thus, Emily's Holyoke experience gave her a sense of inadequacy, inferiority that she could never overcome. She always tried to find excuses for remaining away from services. In 1852 she wrote :

> "They will all go but me to the usual meeting houses, to hear the usual sermons, the inclemency of the storm so kindly detaining me".[8] Such remarks on the part of Emily Dickinson clearly depict that she was overpowered by a strong sense of inferiority complex among her friends and hence she was bound to be a recluse.

In such an environment, Emily trained her young mind with religion. At the age of sixteen, she was lamenting her failure to make her peace with god and asking a friend to pray for her. But certainly thoughts of religion did not darken her life. She could well adjust herself under such circumstances. Rather this inability to become a Christian gave a new dimension to her character and mental set-up and her introspective view of thoughts still deepened.

Like most of her friends, Emily passed many hours in gardening, practicing on piano. Sewing was an exasperation and as far as cleaning the house her attitude was summed up in saying - "I prefer pestilence". The garden however was Emily's special province. She possessed a natural affinity for flowers and always had them about her.

It was almost impossible for a plant to die even a woodland plant, when she had once taken it under her care. She possessed an uncanny knack of making even the frailest growing things flourish under hands. Lilies were great favourite with her. Once she put two day-lilies in the hand of a stranger as her "introduction".

Thus Emily Dickinson, whose story of life is very nearly a blank, remained at home, tending her garden. Her farthest travels consisted of several visits to Boston twice in later years for the care of her eyes, and a short trip to Washington and Philadelphia when she was twenty three. If anytime she fell upon the thorns of life, she was careful that no one should hurt her. For the last twenty years that she lived, she preferred the seclusion of her father's house to any society that village or the world could offer. To intimate friends she sent vivid letters and occasional bits of verse but not even the members of her family suspected the work that she was perfecting in secret. Fame she thought a perilous food and for her own part she would not nibble of it. Only after her death her board of poems uncovered then as increment after increment was published, lovers of poetry gradually came to realize that the most memorable lyric poet in America had lived and died unknown.

Thus Emily Dickinson attended Amherst Academy and was for a year a student at Mary Lyon's Female Seminary at South Hadley. As shown in the family letters and diaries of that period the Dickinson house was overflowed with young life, Emily playing a vivid part in it all, giving no hint of her later seclusion. She visited Worcesters and Boston, and in 1854, when her father was a member of congress, went to Washington, where her wit and intelligence were quickly remarked.

It was during her visit to Philadelphia on her way home, that, in the words of her closest contemporaries "Emily met her fate".[9] According to them, two predestined souls recognized each other - the man a powerful preacher, a scholar, a poet, already married. The inevitable renunciation followed. Its effect, however, was to be enduring. In the old familiar places and ways, she took up her life again, not choosing to withdraw from the world - at least not all at once nor definitely at first - but gradually irresistibly, as her own work and premonition drew her. Her poems became her absorbing passion, those poems from whose publication. She recoiled, and which were only made known to the world after her death. Such an introvert personality as she was, she never wished to be in the limelight through the publication of her poems. She seems to be well acquainted with the transitory nature of the glare of publicity and fame :

> Fame is the one that does not stay –
> Its occupant must die[10]

And again she sings :

> Fame, is a fickle food upon a shifting plate whose table once a guest but not the second time is set[11]

Emily Dickinson in her later years has so often been pictured as a kind of New England nun that an exaggerated impression of her retirement has been created. It was neither abruptly begun nor was it at first abnormal. From the time of her return from Mount Holyoke seminary until her death she lived quietly in her father's house.

Emily did not at once become a recluse. During her twenties, she moved to village society as an introspective young woman. She was sensitive to stars in church, shy of casual meetings and impatient of formalities. She was fond of solitary walks with her big brown dog Carlo.

She herself writes about her shy temperament and self-imposed imprisonment, where she has well-adjusted herself and has no desire to change :

I years had been from home,
And now, before the door,
I dared not open, lest a face
I never saw before
stare vacant into mine
And ask my business there

. . . .

I fumbled at my nerve,
I scanned the windows near
The silence like an ocean rolled
And broke against my ear

. . . .

I fitted to the latch
My hand, with trembling case
Lest back the awful door should spring,
and leave me standing there.[12]

It is not clear just when Emily Dickinson began to dress invariably in white and to invert herself in an atmosphere of hallowed mystery that her garments symbolized. By 1862, her retirement from the world had become marked but not absolute.

By 1870, her seclusion had become a conscious resolution, "I do not cross my father's ground to any house or town." For the last fifteen years of her life the village knew Emily Dickinson only as a white figure flitting about the garden in the summer dust.

The village at first considered her an invalid and latterly pronounced her "gifted but queer". Friends of the family thought her an exquisite touch me not and considerably avoided any intrusion on Miss Dickinson's privacy.

Emily Dickinson had tried society and the world and found them lacking. She was not an invalid and she lived in seclusion from no love,—disappointment. Her life was normal blossoming of a nature, introspective to a high degree, whose best thought could not exist in pretence. She let her thought and feeling slip in her accustomed groves. Emily shut herself behind that austere but tonic hemlock hedge and made her house a nunnery. We imagine to hear her voice singing –

The soul selects her own sovity -

Then - Shuts the Door -[13]

The most dramatic event in her external life started occurring in 1858 and 1859 when she began to seclude herself from the outside world. She had begun a process of withdrawl. She writes :

Deprived of other Banquet
I entertained Myself -
At first - a scant nutrition
An insufficient loaf-[14]

Then came the drama of her inner life. In 1885, her suppressed energies were released, suddenly fully, even frightingly released. To Emily, seclusion was a necessary condition for creativity; If her personal behaviour was mad, then the madness was at least a productive aberration - very close to genius.

The explanation for Emily Dickinson's self-exile is simply not to be found in biographical data alone. We must look directly to the poetry if we hope to fathom the last thirty years of Emily's life and the increasingly neurotic behaviour to which those years were given over. One concludes eventually that if poems were Emily Dickinson's letters to the world they likewise constituted her explanation. So we are naturally led to her upstairs bed-room in which a uniquely private poet found it possible to speak about herself with candour.

The life of seclusion that Emily later led ostensibly does not mean a life of inactivity. The watchwords of the seminary were :

"Do what no one else is willing to do -
go where no one else is willing to go."

Emily fulfilled it in a more subtle way

To fight aloud is very brave,
But gallanter I know
who charge within the bosom
The cavalry of woe[15]

Thus the predominant features shaping Emily's nature, temperament, outlook, were a zest for living and a love for her home. The attachment to her family and her home had become so compulsive at the time when she was twenty-one years of age, that she declined an invitation to visit Jane Hamphrey even for a week:

> I am afraid I am growing selfish in my dear home, but I do love it so when some pleasant friend invites me to pass a week with her. I look at my father and mother. I say "no, no, I cannot leave them what if they die when I am gone".[16]

The first of the huge negations that separated her from the accepted forms of action in her time and by so doing forced her into individual activities of her own occurred while she was at the seminary. There she discovered that she could not share the religious life of her generation. One outlet was forever closed to her, not because she lacked religious feelings. For better or worse, she left impelled to turn aside from the way of truth as her contemporaries understood it. Hers was to be a career of exploration, not of far off islands but of the desert places in the human soul:

"Abiah, you may be surprised to hear me speak as I do, knowing that I express no interest in the all-important subject but I am not happy and I regret that last term when the golden opportunity was mine that I did not give up and become a Christian. It is not now too late, so my friends tell me, so my offended conscience whispers, but it is not hard for me to give up the world .....I am one of the lingering bad ones and so do I shirk away and pause and ponder and ponder and pause and .... you know of this depth and fullness, will you try to tell me about it."[17]

This compulsion became an obsession in her late twenties. Moreover, her father imposed strict restruction for visiting and moving away from her home. For her father, Emily Dickinson felt a respect akin to awe since her early childhood. Before she was twenty, she had come to realize that her father was the shaping force of her nature and personality. Such strictness on the part of Emily's father bred in her shyness to an extreme degree. Once a stranger knocked at the door, Emily Dickinson went to open it but due to extreme shyness, she dared not face the stranger and she hastely retreated into the interior of the house. Mr. Conrad Aiken remarked; "that Miss Dickinson became a hermit by deliberate and conscious choice."[18]

It would be wrong to interpret that Emily's seclusion evolved from her disappointment in love. In fact, there are a number of complex interior factors, social and religious, personal which bred introspective tendency in the mental faculties of Emily Dickinson :

> All pity for Emily Dickinson's 'starved-life' is misdirected. Her life was one of the richest and deepest ever lived on the continent. She went upstairs closed her door and mastered life and world by rejecting it.[19]

Writing poetry in her upstairs room of her home relieved Emily Dickinson from the burden of emotions that surged within herself and which if not found outlet through poetry, would have broken her completely. She realized that the strange flame of poetry which was burning within, had to be nourished by the oil of the inner soul, protected from any external droughts, which might extinguish it. Thus she withdrew herself from the world outside, lived the life of a poetic hermit or recluse, dedicated herself completely to poetry with greater earnestness and singleness.

At the age of twenty-one, in one of her letters to Jane Hamphrey, she wrote how her imagination led her to pretend that she saw herself in her own coffin. Thus since her early childhood she loved to live alone, which turned the flow of thoughts, feelings and emotions inward and her temperament turned out to be increasingly introspective. What she lacked in social life, she gained in secluded life. She did not reject life because of her disappointment in love affair. But she did so in order to find clue to the fundamental problems i.e. man's relation with nature, God, death and what lay beyond death. Hence Emily Dickinson's secluded existence leading the life of an introvert recluse, enriched her scope of introspection and provided her divine zeal. Although Dickinson lived secluded life, her letters reveal knowledge of the writings of John Keats, John Ruskin, and Sir Thomas Browne. Most important writers for her were Shakespeare, Elizabeth Browning, Charlotte and Emily Bronte, George Eliot, and George Sand. Her emotional life remains mysterious, despite much speculation about a possible disappointed love affair. Two candidates have been presented: Reverend Charles Wadsworth, with whom she corresponded, and Samuel Bowles, editor of the *Springfield Republican,* to whom she addressed many poems. In 1861-62 she had a crisis; it is not known if she ever fully recovered. Wadsworth had moved to San Francisco and Bowles disappointed her by traveling in 1861 to Europe. He returned in Autumn 1862. At that time Dickinson did not want to meet him or write to him any more. Her father died in 1874 and mother in 1882. During this period Judge Otis Lord, a friend and colleague of her father, brought some love into Dickinsons's life. Lord was a widower and 18 years her senior.

Emily Dickinson suffered acutely from a lack of intellectual companionship and she existed in a vacuum. She came to be regarded as eccentric. But the fact remains that she grew up normally enough with good schooling, much letter-writing, boy-friends, gardening and household work. Her day-to-day life cannot be understood in such simple terms as a neurotic withdrawl. The house where she lived was filled with relatives and visitors throughout the year. She cooked and cleaned and gardened; she composed drafting and revising letters to a wide circle of friends. Crucially, with the backing of Austin and Benjamin Newton and Susan, she came early to know that she was a poet, so that when the crisis came in 1861 and 1862 she sustained herself writing a poem a day. During 1861-1864, she wrote over 750 poems, such a rate of poems not only demands a heavy spending of psychic energy, it must have also yielded her "a radiant happiness" within the heart of her misery.

Emily Dickinson did not write for publication but for herself or more rarely for friends. Her poems were found after her death by her sister. Her poetry is that of a recluse and mystic but a recluse without any trace of the morbid or inhuman element. We find her continually on the threshold of wonder, standing detached in the sudden realization of the greatness of little things. The Winter of 1861-62 was the sharpest psychic corner in Emily Dickinson's life. Her dream palace was suddenly left tenantless. In desperate earnest she began to write poems and though no man could ever be to her again what her departed master had been. From this time may be dated her withdrawal from the world. Perhaps as a poet she could find the fulfilment she had missed as a woman. She elected to sink deeper and deeper into seclusion and steadily declined to let her poems be printed. Her indifference to publication is a point of apparent abnormality that demands careful attention :

"How dreary to be Somebody
How public like a frog
To tell your name the livelong day
To an admiring bog !"[20]

Did she not loathe the least taint of commercialism?

"Publication is the auction
of the mind of man
Poverty be justifying
For so foul a thing"[21]

Principal Published Works

During her life of seclusion, Emily Dickinson became more and more absorbed in writing poetry, but she showed no desire to publish her poems. She enclosed some of them with letters. Fortunately her family realized the unusual quality of her works and after her death arranged to have collected and published.

Poems, (1886)
Poems : Second Series (1896)
Poem : Third Series (1914)
Further Poems (1929)
Unpublished Poems (1936)
Bolts of Melody : New Poems (1945)
The Poems of Emily Dickinson (1955)

But only six of her poems appeared in print before her death; one mutilation of these by zealous editors who wanted to 'correct' her vagaries of rhyme, meter and punctuation was a factor in her decision not to see publication but to take her chances with fame after death. Well meaning editing continued to haunt her work long after she died and only recently, in *The Poems of Emily Dickinson*, edited by Thomas H. Johnson and published in three volumes in 1955, has the world been allowed to read her lyrics as she wrote and punctuated them.

Poetry was Emily's playmate through years of loneliness. In the seclusion of her father's house while she tended her flowers or performed her share of the household routine, she matched with breathless intentness the motions of her mind, so curiously a part of her and yet aloof. A number of her best poems were certainly in existence in the early sixties among them "Safe in their alabaster Chambers".

As a poet she exhibited the following characteristics :

1. natural feelings
2. themes of hope, fear, time, etc.
3. Paradoxical personality
4. imperfect rhyme-schemes
5. poetic conceits in the manner of Donne
6. Emersonian sense of harmony in nature
7. mystic poetic genius
8. ironic vision
9. individualism
10. death-obsession or 'graveyardism'
11. extreme iconoclasm
12. pleasure-pain antithesis

Conrad Aiken rightly remarks when he states that if we seek the causes of Emily Dickinson's injury which so sharply turned her in upon herself, we can only speculate. Her letters in this regard give little light, only showing us again and again that the injury was deep. One of the fact that she suffered acutely from intellectual drought, there is evidence enough. She is discrete, pathetic, baffled a little humbled and draws in her horns, takes sometimes a perverse pleasure in indulging more than ever, on the occasion of such disappointment. The problems of good and evil, of life and eath, destiny of human soul and the mysteries of nature, this world and hereafter obsessed her perpetually. She writes:

> The soul unto itself
> Is an imperial friend -
> Or the most agonizing spy
> An enemy could send.
> Secure against its own
> No treason it can fear,
> Itself its sovereign, of itself
> The soul should stand in awe.[22]

Thus for Emily Dickinson, there were three world and she lived in all of them .... There was the world of nature, the things and creatures she saw, heard and felt about; there was the world of "estate", that is the world of friendship and there was the world of the unseen, unheard whence we trail clouds of glory.[23]

Her attitude to love, death and God establish her as a Puritan. Critics have estimated Dickinson as a reclusive and conservative person. Probably, she was a puritan by choice and circumstance. The one point of accepting death as the ultimate goal of life in a fatalistic manner recalls her puritanical bias.

Emily Dickinson by selecting her own society, "shut the door to her divine majority" and there she felt "safer" with just her soul upon the window pane

> Where other creatures put their eyes -
> Incautious - of the sun.[24]

She died at the age of fifty-five on May 15, 1886. She had suffered from Bright's disease from 1884. 'I almost wish there was no Eternity', she had written in her youth, 'To think that we must forever live and never cease to be'. After Dickinson's death her poems were brought out by her sister Lavinia. She co-edited three volumes from 1891 to 1896. Despite its editorial imperfections, the first volume became popular. In the early decades of the twentieth century, Martha Dickinson Bianchi, the poet's niece, transcribed and published more poems, and in 1945 'Bolts of Melody' essentially completed the task of bringing Dickinson's poems to the public. The publication of Thomas H. Johnson's edition of Emily Dickinson's poems finally gave readers a complete and accurate text. His work was not easy as the author had left alternative versions of words, lines and sometimes of whole poems. Johnson found a valuable assistant in Theodora Ward, who was then completing an edition of Dickinson's letters to her grand parents. As editor of Emily Dickinson's Selected Poems (1924) Conrad Aiken (1889-1973) was largely responsible for establishing that poet's posthumous literary reputation.

REFERENCE

1. Sculley Bradley, *The American Tradition in Literature* (New York, Groset and Dunlop Inc., 1967), pp. 1010-1011.
2. Martha Dickinson Bianchi and Alfred Leete Hampson (eds.) Poems by Emily Dickinson, Introduction by Alfred Leete Hampson Boston, (Little Brown and Co. 1952), p. 6.
3. F. Whicker George, *This was a poet: A critical Biography of Emily Dickinson* (New York, Charles Scribner's Sons, 1938).
4. Thomas H. Johnson, *Emily Dickinson: An Interpretive Biography* (Harvard University Press, Belknap Press, 1955), pp. 10-11.
5. *Ibid.*, pp. 13-14.
6. *Ibid.*
7. *Idem.*
8. Johnson, *op. cit.*, p. 14.
9. Martha Dickinson Bianchi Emily Dickinson Face to Face (Houghton Mifflin Company), p. 48.
10. Thomas H. Johnson, *The Complete Poems of Emily Dickinson,* Poem No. 1475 (Kalyani Publishers, Delhi, 1960, p. 623).
11. *Ibid.*, Poem No. 1659, (p. 678).
12. *Ibid.*, Poem No. 609, (p. 299).
13. *Ibid.*, Poem No. 303, (p. 143).
14. *Ibid.*, Poem No. 773, (p. 377).
15. *Ibid.*, Poem No. 126, (p. 59).
16. Thomas H. Johnson, *Emily Dickinson: An Interpretative Biography,* (Harvard University Press, 1967), p. 24.
17. George F. Whicker, *This was a Poet: A Critical Biography of Emily Dickinson*, New York, (1938).

18. Caesar R. Blake and Carlton F. Walls, *The Recollection of Emily Dickinson*. The selected criticism since 1890 (The University of Michigein Press, 1964), p. 157.
19. *Ibid*., p. 158.
20. Johnson, Poem No. 288, p. 133.
21. *Ibid*., Poem No. 709, p. 348.
22. *Ibid*., Poem No. 683, p. 338.
23. Thomas J. Johnson, *Emily Dickinson: An interpretative Biography* (Harvard University Press, 1967), p. 3.
24. Johnson, Poem No. 327, p. 155.

TREATMENT OF NATURE

2

This is my letter to the world
That never wrote to me -
The simple News that Nature told -
With tender Majesty
Her message is committed
To hands I cannot see -
For love of her - Sweet - countrymen -
Judge tenderly - of me,[1]

Since the closing decade of the eighteenth century, nature has been one of the most recurrent themes of English and American poetry. The chief exponent of this subject. William Wordsworth, explored its utmost philosophical limits and in doing so set a trap of convention for the succeeding generations of poets. From him down to the Victorian poets in England and through them to Boyant and Emerson in America, every poet faithfully and at times exasperatingly echoed some of the notable aspects of his attitude towards nature. Wordsworth's pervading influence had so deeply penetrated the literary sensibility of his age that for a long time to come, poets could not get out of the rut, it was almost impossible for them to break away from a tradition, whose validity had achieved widespread acceptance.

Thus it was Wordsworth, (the 'harbinger of Nature' the high-priest of nature and the 'worshipper of nature,' as he is variously called,) who for the first time in English poetry, penetrated beneath the outword manifestation of nature and gave to her a separate life and soul of her own. He spiritualized nature and made her a moral teacher, this is his originality and this is his most important contribution. As Compton - Rickett puts it :

> It was Wordsworth's aim as a poet to seek for beauty in meadow, woodland and the mountain, and to interpret this beauty in spiritual terms. He is ever spiritualizing the moods of 'Nature' and winning from them moral consolation.

This spiritual conception of Nature, however, did not come at once. Wordsworth himself tells us in *The Prelude* and in *Tintern Abbey* that there were four stages in the development of his love for the outer world. In the first stage, his love for nature was without any spiritual or mystical touch. It was like a healthy boy's love of the open air and freedom of the fields :

> ...... when like a roe
> I bounded o'er the mountain, by the sides
> Of the deep rivers and the lonely stream,
> Wherever nature led: .....[2]

In the second stage, he loved nature with a passion which was all physical, without having any tinge of intellectual or philosophical association. It was purely his sensuous love for nature when

> The sounding cataract
> Haunted me like a passion, the tall rook
> The mountain and the deep gloomy woods.[3]

But with the French Revolution "dizzy joys" and "aching raptures" of Nature came to an end and the poet realized the sorrow and sufferings, tears and turmoils of human life. And now he could hear in Nature.

"The still sad music of humanity"[4] And finally he experiences the presence of God colouring all the objects of Nature, inverting them with a celestial light - a light that never was on sea or land. This soul of all the worlds immanent in nature, inspired him with elevated thoughts :

> And I have felt
> A presence that disturbs me with the joy
> of elevated thoughts, and sense sublime
> of something far more deeply interfused .....

\- - - - -

A motion and a spirit, that imples
All thinking things, all objects of all thought
And rolls through all things.[5]

The whole of the universe thus becomes for the poet permeated by one life, one soul, irradiating the thousand manifestations of nature. The spirit of God is everywhere, wherever the poet may go, he has vision of the divine spirit unfolded in the objects of nature.

Thus man, Nature and God were no longer separate entities and man's relation to Nature and God assumes a well-defined pattern as he was merged with the universal being. Wordsworth endows every object of nature with life. He forestalls the modern biological researchers that there is a soul and a living principle in all the forms and shapes of nature's myriad objects:

The highly sensitive and creative mind of Emily Dickinson must have definitely been influenced by the nature poetry of Wordsworth. She, while sitting in her little solitary world, at the window pane, observed every minute object of nature with her keen power of observation and gave an outlet to her microscopic power of imagination. She expresses in the following poem how she feels towards the objects of Nature:

Several of nature's people
I know and they know me
I feel for them a transport
Of cordiality.[6]

The poem quoted below serves as an excellent example to illustrate Dickinson's attitude towards Nature, which very much seems to coincide with that of Wordsworth's:

Nature, the gentlest mother,
Impatient of no child
The feeblest or the waywardest -
Her admonition mild.

\- - - - - -

When all the children sleep
She turns as long away

As will suffice to light her lamps
Then bending from the shy,
with infinite affection
With infinite care,
Her golden finger on her lip
Wells silence everywhere.[7]

Thus to Miss Dickinson, Nature appears as the gentlest mother, very affectionate, loving and care taking soothing and comforting her bruised children. Similarly Wordsworth declares that nature leads from Joy to Joy and brings food for future years. To him Nature is :

The anchor of my purest thoughts, the nurse
The guide - the guardian of my heart and soul
Of all my moral being.[8]

The common objects of nature, like changes in the season, the sun-set and the sun-rise, birds, flowers, wind and the storm fascinated and stirred Emily Dickinson's imagination and filled her with exultation and immense pleasure. She could well sing in tune with William Wordsworth :

To me the meanest flower that blows can give
Thoughts that do often lie too deep for tears.[9]

Emily Dickinson seems to be very anxious and curious for witnessing the bright morning. In such a mood following lines issues from her mind :

Will there really a morning ?
Is there such a thing as day ?
Could I see in from the mountains
If I were as tall as they ?"

- - - - - -

Oh some scholar ! Oh some Sailor !
Oh some wise man from the skies !
Please to tell a little Pilgrim
Where the place called "Morning" lies[10]

The keen and curious eyes of the poetess ultimately catch hold of the glimpse of long-awaited "Morning" and she writes :

The day came slow, till five O'clock
Then sprang before the hills
Like hundred rubies, or the light
A sudden musket spell
The purple could not keep the east
The sunrise shook from fold
Like breadths of topaz, patched a night
The lady just unrolled.[11]

The slow but steady arrival of morning fills the heart of the poetess with immense pleasure and ecstasy. The peaceful and tranquil moments of morning give her soothing and consoling impact like the Paradise :

The morning lit, the birds arose,
The monster's faded eyes
Turned slowly to his native coast,
And peace was Paradise ![12]

In another poem, Dickinson draws even more concrete picture of the approach of morning, accompanied by the sun :

The sun just touched the Morning
The morning happy thing,
Supposed that He had come to dwell
And life would be all spring.[13]

But her clear and sharp perception and insight enable her to notice the inevitable change taking place in the world of nature. And in the following lines she personifies morning fluttering and staggering 'for her crown':

The morning fluttered, staggered
Felt feebly for her crown -
Her unanointed forehead
Henceforth her only one.[14]

Dickinson's minute observation of Nature led her to present image after image to describe various objects of nature. Sometimes she reacts to the day break and morning breeze in the following way :

By and by the boldest stole out of his covert
To see if time was there

Nature was in her beryl apron
Mixing fresher air,[15]

While sitting in her solitary room at the window-pane, Dickinson gave an outlet to her fancy and imagination and perceived the dramatic element in the world of nature. The same dramatic element is visible in the following lines :

Angels in the early morning
May be seen the dews among
stooping, plucking, smiling, flying
Do the buds to them belong ?
Angels when the sun is hottest
May be seen the sands among
Stooping, plucking, sighing, flying
Perched the flowers they bear along.[16]

A minute observer of Nature as Dickinson was, nothing of Nature escaped her notice. Among the natural phenomena she greatly admired were the sun-rise and the sun-set :

I'll tell you how the sun-rose -
A ribbon at a time
The steeples swarm in amethyst
The news like squirrel ran.

\- - - - -

But how he set, I know not
There seems a purple stile
Which little yellow boys and girls
Were climbing all the while.[17]

In the above poem, Emily Dickinson uses a series of action - verbs and domestic images to convey the quick surprise and changing colours of the dawn. A better poem on the same subject opens with an arresting conceit :

Blazing in gold and quenching in purple
Leaping like leopards to the sky
Then at the feet of the old horizon
Laying her spotted face, to die;
Stopping as low as the kitchen window
Touching the roof and tinting the barn,

Kissing her bonnet to the meadow -
And the juggler of day is gone ![18]

In the above poem, Dickinson has sketched photographically the dramatic element present in the nature world. Similarly in the following poem her vivid description of nature is worth noting :

The skies can't keep their secret !
They tell it to the hills -
The hills just tell the orchards -
And they the daffodils !
A Bird by chance, that goes that way
Soft overheard the whole
If I should bribe the little bird
who knows but she would tell ?[19]

The above poem depicts how the poetess, riding on the viewless-wings of imagination, soars higher and higher and transports the reader to the divine world of nature. The reader, as a result, shares the secrets of nature with other objects of nature. How the early glittering rays of the sun, spread its secret message to the hills and mountains, the woods and orchards and they in turn to the daffodils. Luckily a bird, passing by that way, happened to overhear the whole and the poetess got anxious and inquisitive to know it, by giving bribe to the bird but finally she consoles herself and gives up the hope to know the secret of 'new fashioned world'.

So keep your secret, Father !
I would not, if I could,
Know what the sapphire follows do,
In your new fashioned world ![20]

The attention and the imagination of the poetess seem to chase very closely the change taking place every second in the lap of nature.

Dickinson seems to be deeply influenced and fascinated by the magical movement of the rotation of day and night. Everything in the world of nature is in a state of flux; nothing is static, everything keeps changing.

The dramatic occurrences of summer-rains and lightning storms impressed Dickinson equally. The uncontrollable power of these storms, with their complete dominion over man's world, gave her a sense of 'Circumference' and religious fear which deepened their picturesque effect.

The wind begun to rock the grass
With threatening tunes and low -
He flung a menace at the earth,
A menace at the sky.[21]

The poem quoted above employs touches of local colour which, together with a fantastic array of action-verbs, exhibits the mysterious chaos of a sudden summer downpour. Similarly

There came a wind like a Bugle
It quiversed through the grass
And a green chill upon the heat ....[22]

The above lines, extracted from a later storm-poem, enlarge the feeling of reverence and surprise that any life can survive such onslaughts. We note a sharp distinction between the early and the later period of Emily Dickinson's poetic career especially the poems dealing with the theme of nature. In the early phase of her writing, she could concentrate only on the external phenomena of natural world and like romantic poets, she picked up any object of nature and admired and appreciated in her verse. In the following beautiful poem on 'flower', her heart aches at the worthless, useless unknown unadmired life of beautiful flowers, which grow and perish unnoticed :

How many flowers fail in wood
Or perish from the hill
Without the privilege to know
That they are beautiful !
How many cast a nameless post
Upon the nearest breeze
Unconscious of the scarlet freight
It bears to other eyes ![23]

Emily Dickinson, in the above poem, sympathises with the obscure fate of those flowers which bloom and blossom, without knowing their own worth and value that they are beautiful. The given poem brings to our mind the famous lines of *Gray's Elggy Written in A Country Churchyard* :

Full many a gem of purest ray serene
The dark, unfathomed caves of ocean bear
Full many a flower is born to blush unseen
And waste its sweetness on the desert air.

There is yet another poem dealing with the same theme which shows Emily Dickinson's deep-rooted sympathy with the objects of nature :

The mountains grow unnoticed
Their purple figure rise
Without attempt, exhaustion
Assistance or applause.[24]

The description of the hesitant, almost tentative approach of the spring season, the sudden blossoming forth of the leaves and flowers delight Emily Dickinson, Spring received ampler treatment in another poem in which each line gives separate characteristics of spring season :

A wider sunrise in the morn -
A deeper twilight on the lawn -
A print of a vermilion foot -
A purple finger on the slope -[25]

The same theme is repeated in another poem where valley, the hills, the trees are swept clean and are given what in modern cliché is called "face-left" in honour of the visiting spring :

The tidy Breeze, with their Brooms
Sweep vale - and hill - and tree !
Prethee my Pretty Housewives
Who may expected by ?[26]

The neighbours do not know the answer but the woods knowingly exchange a smile :

And yet, how still the landscape stands
How nonchalant the Hedge !
As if the Resurrection
Were nothing very strange[27]

Again in the following poem, Dickinson repeats the idea in her characteristically witty manner :

Spring is the Period
Express from God
Among other seasons
Himself abide.
But during March and April
None stir abroad
Without a cordial interview
With God[28]

In other seasons God abides by Himself and it is only the spring season which He especially ordains and manifestly comes down to reveal His glory all round with its profound impact on discerning eyes. Another variant of the same theme is embodied in another poem :

A light exists in spring
Not present on the year
At any other period -
When March is scarcely here[29]

This poem is perhaps Miss Dickinson's best analysis of the peculiar awe that the season of spring inspires. Spring was Miss Dickinson's favourite season, such it displayed the wonder of rebirth and openly promised the warm beauty of summer. She calls spring a time, sent directly from God and particularly welcomed March as the herald of spring. It is here she describes March, as the pivot of the new year, when spring transforms the cold barren winter. Spring's hope is compared to a rarely glimpsed light which carries regent and religious associations to signify the psychological insights that occur at such a moment. This illumination heightens man's emotional awareness of spring's mysteries and enlarges his poignant sense of estrangement.

In the final stanza of the same poem, the poetess states the significance of the experience emphasizing its religious value and desolation that follows its departure :

A quality of loss
Affecting our content

As trade had suddenly encroached
upon a Sacrament.[30]

The return of reality harshly phrased as "trade" typifies the proceeding of a large impersonal company interested only in measurable gain and unconcerned about religious intangibles. The moment's sacramental aspects, displaying God's grace and power are now lost. Throughout the poem, motion and light images are constantly inter-woven to suggest the longing and awe that the light brings. Thus the physical experience of a day in early spring is transformed into a moment of religious illumination.

In the following poem, Dickinson's love and absorption in the objects of nature is vividly perceptible.

An altered look about the hills;
A wider sunrise in the morn;
A deeper twilight on the lawn;
- - - -
All this and more I cannot tell[31]

Thus from light local-colour sketches, as in the above poem, she moves to more and more thoughtful consideration of the whole cycle of seasons in "New Feet within my garden go".

"New feet within my garden go,
New fingers stir the sod,
- - - - -
New children play upon the green
New weary sleep below;
And still the pensive spring returns
And still the punctual snow !"[32]

As the time goes on, the light existing in spring, slowly but steadily disappears, leaving it dull, monotonous and 'pensive'.

The light that Dickinson speaks of is not the visionary gleam seen by the mystics. It is a colour which cannot be perceived by scientific observation but can only be felt by those who have matched the change of seasons with loving care. The spring and the summer seasons were the most stimulating and inspired a large number of her poems. Even when winter lay bare all around her, she was comforted with the thought of 'Summer':

It will be Summer eventually
Ladies with parosoles
Sauntering gentlemen with canes,
And little girls with dolls
Will tent the pallid landscape
As't were a bright banquet.
- - - - -
Till summer folds her miracle
As women do their gown:[33]

This is wrong to suppose that since Emily Dickinson had cut herself adrift from the long tradition of nature poetry bequeathed to her generation by Wordsworth, it may seem that she did not have much to write about. On the contrary, she wrote more than 500 poems on nature and there is hardly any of nature's creature under the sun, and within her physical reach which escaped her attention. For obvious reasons, her major themes were the seasons and the elemental forces which brought about a change.

Emily Dickinson used to go out on picnic parties in her girlhood. She gradually withdrew to her garden house, and finally to her room from where she observed the outer world. From an ample crack in the window curtain, she saw the branch of the apple tree :

Like a Venetian - waiting
Accosts my open eye -[34]

And on this bough is seen the "Emerakle" of summon and the "Diamonds" of winter snow. In one of her early poems, she introduces spring season thus :

Baffled for just a day or two -
Embarrassed - not afraid -
Encounter in my garden -
An unexpected Maid.[35]

How minutely she watches the change occurring in the world of nature :

Dear March, come in !
How glad I am !
I looked for you before,
Put down your hat -
You must have walked -
How cut of breath you are !
Dear March, how are you ?
\- - - - -
Who knocks ? That April !
Look the door ![36]

She reacts to changing season differently. While she welcomes March, she is not prepared to show any hospitality to April. She draws affinity between the activities of children and the movements of beautiful flowers.

An children bid the guest good-night,
And then reluctant turn,
My flowers raise their petty lips
Then put their nightgowns on
An children caper when they wake
Merry that it is morn,
My flowers from a hundred cribs,
Will peep, and prance again[37]

It absolutely startles one to find among the memorials of this secluded life, a picture so vividly objective and clear-cut as this :

Glee - The great storm is over -
Four - have recovered the land -
Forty - gone down together -
Into the toiling sand[38]

Very few poets could draw a sea-picture in stronger lines than this secluded woman, Miss Dickinson.

She was fascinated by the phenomena of nature, by the variety of its colour and sound and with her characteristic analytical mind, she explored the complex implications of her experience. In this, as in various other respects, she anticipated the modern attitude which refers to make up any facile assignment of man in relation to the cosmos and views nature as something shorn of all sentimentality. It would be wrong to believe, however, that Emily Dickinson did not occasionally slip into the prevalent convention of transcendentalism but more often than not her conventional thinking was coloured by the whimsy of her thought and expression.

Dickinson, however, never claimed to have understood the deep mystery of the phenomena of nature. Even though gifted with acute power of observations and the intensely sensitive mind of a great artist, she did not succeed in entering the innermost sanctuary of Nature. For her, Nature and God were two unknowable entities, which were beyond the range of human knowledge. She did not pretend to read ultimate meanings in Nature. For her, nature was an endless carnival of entertainment. It was also a source of metaphor to illustrate the truths of her interviewed world.

The external loveliness of the forests and the hills are only the outer fringe of the tent, like traveling the circus, nature has installed and it would be a grave error to mistake the outside for the inside :

> We spy the Forests and the Hills
> The Tents to Nature's show
> Mistake the outside for the in
> And mention what we saw.[39]

Again, Dickinson argues in another poem that nature is 'sedate' at times and 'grand' on other occasion, but our observation should end there, as nature's practices extend to necromancy:

> To Necromancy and the Trades
> Remote to understand
> Behold our spacious citizen
> Unto "juggler turned
> Unto "juggler turned-[40]

Dickinson was cramped by the limitations of her expression to delineate in words. Like Mr. T.S. Eliot who emerged on the poetic scene almost a century later, she also felt the inadequacy of words, not only in the formulation of philosophical abstractions but also even in the communication of what senses perceived.

Nature is what we see
The Hill - the Afternoon
Nay - Nature is heaven—
Nature is what we hear

- - - - -

Nay, Nature is Harmony
Nature is what we know
Yet have no art to say
So impotent our wisdom is
To her Simplicity.[41]

Nature's ostensible simplicity and artlessness is deceptive and conceals the illusive complexity which we have neither the discerning wisdom nor the competence of art to describe.

Emily Dickinson's departure from romanticism was thus complete. In rejecting the Emersonian assumption of merging of man, nature and God, she went a step further to ridicule the transcendentalists in one of her poems.

A little madness in the spring
Is wholesome even for the king.[42]

By rejecting Emersonian tradition, Emily Dickinson set of different task for her as a poet. She could no longer indulge in rambling generalization but had to pie down her perception as well as its delineation in the most precise words. She had a search for vocabulary which could evoke the transcient moods and elusive truth. It was not only half to perceive and half to create, it was to perceive fully and recreate faithfully in words.

Sometimes, Emily Dickinson declares her monopoly over the enjoyment of the attractions of nature and exclaims in a mood of superiority over other human beings :

The sun went down -
No man looked on,
The earth and I alone
Were present at the majesty[43]

Not only this, she goes to the extent of saying :

Heaven has different sign to me
Sometime I think that noon
Is but a symbol of the place
- - - -
All there remind us of the place
The men call "Paradise[44]

But she believes that human belings are not endowed with such deeper and keener sensibility to watch and realize the hidden secrets of nature and enjoy the "Beauty" which is nothing else but Truth"

Beauty is not caused - it is;
Chase it and it ceases
chase it not and it abides.[45]

The poetess feels proud of herself because she can look deeper in the heart of things and can share the moods of nature :

My faith is larger than the hills
So when the hills decay
My faith must take the purple which
To show the sun the way.[46]

Emily Dickinson must have been familiar with Wordsworth. The spectacle of nature did not urge her to philosophize on her own or on human predicament and more than anything else it was for her a feast for the eye which she hopes to recreate in her poetry. She loves the natural world, her earthly paradise, for its winds and storms, its black-bees, its robin which eats its worm raw, the snake in its boggy acre, bats and rats, and spiders, the humming - bird and fifty other creatures, sights, sounds and sensations. If we attempt to summarize the poet's responses to natural sights and phenomena, it excites a feeling of wonder in us. "What mystery pervades a well" is a poem in which images of the deep well and "floorless sea" lead to the following comment -

But nature is a stranger yet
The ones that cites her most

Have never passed her haunted house
Nor simplified her ghost.
To pity those that know her not
Is helped by the regret
That those who know her, know her less
The nearer her they get.[47]

Dickinson has very vividly depicted her own confused conception of nature in the following little poem.

Not knowing when the dawn will come
I open every door
Or has it features like a bird
Or billows like a shore ?[48]

Some of the romantics, notably Wordsworth and Walt Whitman, had turned to the homely aspects of the natural scene, but it was either to find God in natural objects or to preach the democracy of all created things. Miss Dickinson found both these philosophies alien. She sought new approaches, as in a group of poems celebrating aristocracy of leisure in Nature's humbler forms.

Dickinson was basically a mystic and a nature poet. Some oppose this idea and call her frame of mind as domestic and even whimsical. This is grossly unfair. In the poem "Behind Me—Dips Eternity" she says :

Behind me - dips Eternity -
Before me - immortality -
Myself - the term between -
Death but the Drift of Eastern Gray.

In "I felt A funeral, in My Brain" She says :

And them a Plane in Reason, broke
And dropped down, and down -
And hit a world, at every plunge
And finished knowing - then -

In one of these she went to the extreme of praising a weed for being unconscious of its low station, at summer's close, sweep "as lightly from disdain/As Lady from her lower" Her poem on grass, usually recorded as merely an amusing is a celebration of the majectic leisure of Nature :

The grass so little has to do -
A sphere of simple green -
With only Butterflies to brood
And Bees to entertain
- - - -
And then to dwell in sovereign barns
And dream the days way,-
The grass so little has to do,
I wish I were a hay ![49]

The treatment of natural object "grass", no matter how insignificant it looks yet Dickinson's thinking and keen observation has made it significant. No doubt, her approach to Nature is unique, and has avoided the theme of Nature - as healer which had grown hackneyed in the poetry of her country.

A companion poem on the pebble, supplements her tribute to grass by emphasizing more insistently Nature's separateness from man : The stone is carefree because it fulfils "absolute decree" Its perfect serenity results from its "simplicity" as with grass. But such happy state of affairs is impossible for human beings. Whose consciousness separates him from this harmony. The stone is utterly contented, and is incapable of feeling alone because it is unconscious :

How happy is the little stone
That rambles in the road alone
And does not care about careers
And exigencies never fears
Fulfilling absolute decree
In casual simplicity.[50]

The poem explores the idea of nature's perfect harmony with Divine plan, and gives us a contrast between the stone's elemental obedience to man's disordered existence. According to Emily Dickinson, the source of the stone's happiness is its self-sufficiency and its refusal to try to exceed its limitations or potential. The poem has a deep tone of irony. Thus even the most insignificant objects of nature fascinated her and sometimes brought to her daring original thoughts.

Gradually a change is perceptible in Emily Dickinson's treatment of nature. Her early period of creation follows the conventional trend of nature poetry, depicting it like the "gentlest mother", soothing and comforting her bruised children. In fact, in these poems she delights in Nature's external pageantry and expresses a sentimental enthusiasm about the red breast of the robin and the beautiful colours of the butterfly. But her later poems show the distrust of such analogies and depict an ironic contrast between nature's ordered majesty with man's doomed mortality. Unlike Wordsworth, her view is that Nature mocks rather than comforts man. Some of her poems analyse Nature's betrayal of those hearts that love her best :

> The morning after woe,
> "Tis frequenty the way,
> Surpasses all that rose before
> For utter jubilee
> As Nature did not care
> And piled her blossoms on,
> The further to parade a joy
> Her victim started upon.[51]

The above poem clearly explains the indifferent part played by Nature. The same vein of thought continues in the following poem :

> I Dreaded that first Robin, so
> But he is mastered now
> But I'm accustomed to him grown -
> He hurts a little, though
> \- - - -
> I dared not meet the daffodils
> For fear their yellow gown
> Would pierce me with a fashion
> So foreign by my own.[52]

Her reaction at the sight of beautiful daffodils stands in sharp contrast to that of Wordsworth who exclaims :

> A poet could not but be gay
> In such a jocund company

I gazed and gazed but little thought
What wealth the show to me had brought

Miss Dickinson's treatment of Nature in her poet distinguished her from other Nature poets. While some of her earlier poems are conventional praise of Nature, as "the gentlest mother" her mature outlook is absolutely different. In one of her Nature poems, "What mystery pervades a well, she examines the mystery and we often associated with a deep well :

What mystery pervades a well !
Use water lives so far.
Like neighbour from another world
Residing in a jar.

- - - -

But nature is a stranger yet :
The ones that cite her most
Have never passed her haunted house,
Nor simplified her ghost.[53]

And finally she concludes the poem by exclaiming—

To pity those that know her not
Is helped by the regret
That those who know her, know her less,
The nearer her they get.[54]

Nature, according to Miss Dickinson, remains mysterious and elusive. The more we scrutinize Nature's processes, the more complex and bewildering they become. Essentially, Nature exists as an alien baffling force that defies full comprehension. Thus her attitude is wide apart from that of visionary pantheists like Wordsworth.

A number of her poems reveal to us the truth that Emily Dickinson's description of nature illuminates her philosophy Her attitude towards nature is something complex and does not fall into a neat philosophy as that of Wordsworth. She had no faith in nature as a guide of formal behaviour while Wordsworth believes :

In nature and in language of sense
The anchor of my purest thought, the nurse,

The guide, the guardian of my heart, and soul
of all my moral being ....

But Emily Dickinson did not share such ideas. No doubt, she has observed the charming and fascinating aspects of nature, yet she is equally well aware of the destructive and corruptive aspects of nature, that is, her attitude to nature is not lop-sided or biased at all. Wordsworth says that Nature never betrays the heart that loves her; but Emily Dickinson finds nature the betrayal of those hearts that love her best and does not always lead from 'joy to joy'. It is where Emily Dickinson stands in sharp contrast with Wordsworth who holds the view that Nature brings 'food for future year'.

Emily Dickinson is pre-occupied with the destructive aspects of Nature. The violent, destructive forces of Nature, like storm, lightning, thunder, attracted her. She had a keen eye for the repulsive, ugly, decaying and corrupting power in nature.

Emily Dickinson deviated from the conventional appreciation of the object of nature and emphasizes the decaying and corruptive power lying hidden in the world of nature. The following poem on such theme is remarkable :

Apparently with no surprise
To any happy flower
The frost beheads it at its play
In accidental power.
The blond assassin passes on
The sun proceeds unmoved
To measure off another day
For an approving God.[55]

In the above poem she describes how mercilessly the frost kills a happy flower. She even questions if Nature has any meaning at all because the universe that proceeds indifferently and is untouched by such crimes haunts one with terror. Similarly in another poem, "A Lady red upon the hill", she concludes by stressing the hostility of nature :

And yet how still the landscape stands
How nonchalant the wood

As if the "resurrection"
Were nothing very odd ![56]

One of the important poems "A Narrow Fellow In the Grass" deals with the terror and awe of snakes in the grass. Like the humming birds, the snake's route is one of instantaneous appearings and disappearings :

A Narrow Fellow in the grass
occasionally rides -
You may have met Him - did you not
His notice sudden is -
- - - -
But never met this fellow
Attended, or alone
Without a tighter breathing
And Zero at the Bone -[57]

Perhaps it is only in this poem that Miss Dickinson treats nature as actively hostile. The above poem offers a rather disturbing investigation of Nature's mystery. Here the poet examines the terror and awe that a snake's presence can cause. A series of artistic progressions develop the snake image into a symbol of the unknown. At first the snake is treated very playfully, his sudden 'notice' and quick moments fascinate the observer and conveys a some of regality and power as his coiling body is compared to a 'whip lash unbraiding the sun'. Thus the image of the snake develops the association with man's fear of the unknown and evil itself. Here the sense of hidden terror behind Nature's surface beauty fascinate and frightens the onlooker. Thus, the above poem on snake effectively draws the attention of the reader to the stark realities of nature in the form of sudden terror behind Nature's external appearance. Wordsworth immense love and adoration for Nature blinded him to such realistic aspect of nature. Thus the poem considers the ambivalence of Nature's beauty and grace having such a destructive core. Beneath its tranquil surface exists a world of a fear and continuous warfare. Dickinson feels that bat is an ugly creature, seems to mock the beauties of nature and writes in an ironic tone :

The Bat is dun, with wrinkled wings-
Like fallow Article -
And not a song pervades his lips
or none perceptible ....
Elate philosopher.[58]

Nothing in the vast range of nature could escape her microscopic notice and her eyes caught view of every single object of nature, not leaving the dark-wrinkled winged bat, roaming about in the dark and silent hours of night. Similarly, the same playful note is struck in another charming poem on an object of nature seldom chosen for conventional poetic treatment. The poem is :

The mushroom is the elf of plants
At evening it is not
At morning in a truffled hut
It stops upon a spot
Is vegetation juggler
The germ of Alibi.[59]

The fantastic comparisons and mock heroic phrase like "vegetation's juggler", germ alibi enhance the humorous effect while underlying the baffling nature of the mushroom seems to defy nature's rules. Thus the above poem on mushroom offers an excellent blend of humour and mysticism. Unlike Wordsworth she found nature to be complex, mysterious, not fully comprehensible, on the whole an alien force. She is endowed with a special capacity to observe nature minutely as is evident from the following description of a bird :

A bird came down the walk
He did not know I saw -
And bit an Angle worm in halves
And ate the fellow raw.
And then he drank a Dew
From a convenient grass -
And them hopped sidewise to the wall
To let a Beetle pass-[60]

In the above poem, Emily Dickinson touches the spring of difference to separate the two words i.e. the world of Nature and the world of man. The remarkable line is - 'He did not know I saw'. As long as the poetess is unobserved, the life of Nature goes on with such spontaneous informality as to give her some hope of participating in it. But Nature is alien to man because the external world is ultimately unknowable by the mind, even its forms vanish before man's eyes.

The poetess observes that the bird's dinner is a worm its drink is 'Dew' taken from a convenient grass; she is left towering about and outside, having no magic to reduce herself to a size or to a level where communication is possible. Bird recognizes its fellow beetle with a show of courtesy; still unaware of the human intruder. As she tends to join in, the bird's eyes become "Frightened beads". But she soon realized "How different we are!" Her failure to establish relations with a winged creature in her garden dramatizes this difference. Thus she sees Nature not only irrevocably separated from man but indifferent to man's feelings and emotions also. She wrote "Nature must be too young to feel or many years too old". This view is in sharp contrast to the Nature poetry of her heritage and this belief underlines her best work.

Thus even though the theme of the poem is trite of hackneyed, yet her manner of rendering it makes it great. Man's spying and his useless offer of 'crumb' lead to the bird's final rejection and illuminates another theme : Nature's superiority and self-sufficiency over man's fumbling awkwardness.

Another well-known Emily Dickinson's bird-poem is the famous eight-line poem on the humming bird, written late in life. Justly admired as a flowless lyric it is also significant in relation to her theory of perception.

A Route of Evanescence
With a revolving wheel -
A resonance of Emerald -
A Rush of cochineal -
And every blossom on the Bush
Adjusts its tumbled Head -
The mail from Tunis, probably
An easy Morning Ride -[61]

Miss Dickinson here represents a humming bird's elusiveness by using the word evanescen meaning "fleeting" or transitory or "Vanishing". She wrote in one of letters in 1880 "All we secure is its evanescence". In the poem the idea of evanescence is rendered in terms of motion, colour and sound. To begin with, the outline of the bird's figure is replaced by its disappearing path across the field of vision. The first line of the poem records not the simultaneous presence but the simultaneous vanishing of the bird at every point.

The concluding lines of the poem are intended to convey the full effect of the bird's flight beyond the barriers of space and time. "Tunis" was a very remote place to her, and an easy morning ride' from there could only have been achieved on a magic carpet in those days.

Thus the above poem is Dickinson's finest achievement as it gives the whole sensation of the humming-bird-first a dazzle of sudden sense impression, movement, motion of wings, colour and whir; all at once then (the birds departure taken for granted) the emptiness emphasized by the clear picture of nodding blossoms and with finally the startled mind of the supposed spectator regaining its poise.

This poem is a striking example of the author's spell in giving concrete expression to abstract ideas, one of her most notable qualities. Thus "A Route of Evanescene" contains Dickinson's most famous Nature - portrait that of the humming-bird, which also conveys the sense of Nature's mystery and elusiveness.

Similarly "Further in summer than the Birds" is a fine example of Miss Dickinson's Nature poetry dealing with the well known insect, the cricket :

> Further in Summer than the Birds
> Pathetic from the grass
> A minor Nation celebrates
> Its unobtrusive Mass . .[62]

The poem shows Dickinson's fascination for Nature's odd creatures and the mysterious passage of summer into winter. She associates the cricket's song with the sadness of seasonal change, as in this poem. Basically the poem records her response to the monotonous chirping of the crickets on a hot August noon, near the end of summer. The image of cricket is transformed into a striking symbol of the estrangement and sorrow that man feels with the approach of winter, an echo of his own intimations of mortality. In a sense, then, their song shows the cleavage of man from Nature. Man can perceive that his isolation is not a unique phenomenon but cosmic and universal.

Summer in New England is associated with rain which washes away the putrid slaughter of winter and hastens the process of recognition in nature. The snow is swept clean, the dead grass sends animated sports and the trees sway with expected loads of foliage flowers and fruits. Rain in summer is thus symbol of the joy of creation and fruitfulness. Dickinson noticed the rejoicing in the element with the advert of rain. In one of her poems. "A Drop fell on the Apple Tree" she catches the mood of summer showers.

> The Dust replaced, in Hoisted Roads -
> The sunshine threw his Hat away -
> The Bushes - sprangles flung -[63]

The rain is often accompanied by the pleasant breeze of summer, sometimes it comes to top at the door like a tired man :

> A Rapid - footless guest
> To offer whom a chair
> were as impossible as hand
> A sofa to the air -[64]

But there are occasions when it comes blowing sand, pebbles, boys hats, and an occasional steeple, with a hoarse cry, "Get out of the way I say". The wind is not always gentle, it often comes on the wings of tumultuous thunder stones Emily Dickinson reproduces the terrifying spectacle of ruthless ferocity.

Even though Miss Dickinson thought Nature to be on the whole an alien force, Nature never ceased to fascinate her. She was no Wordsworthian. She found Nature to be complex, mysterious not fully comprehensible. Yet she delighted in

Nature's external pageantry and felt highly enthusiastic about Nature's colours, grandeur, immensity and diversity. The following poem is an excellent example of Emily Dickinson's enthusiastic response to various objects of Nature, for example, the sky the meadows, the mountains, the forests, the stars, the motions of the dipping birds, "The morning's amber road:"

> Before I got my eye put out
> I liked as well to see -
> - - - - -
> But were it told to me-to-day
> That I might have the sky
> For mine - I tell you that my Heart
> Would split, for size of me
> - - - I could take
> Between my finite eyes -
> The motions of the Dipping Birds -
> The Morning's amber Road -
> For mine - to look at when I liked -
> The News would strike me dead-[65]

Nature's overwhelming impact on her soul is clearly visible in the above poem. This is not a simple sentiment of love for Nature. Miss Dickinson here dwells upon the profundity and infinity of Nature and human soul's incapacity to embrace Nature in all its entirety.

If Dickinson were told that she could have the sky as her own possession, her heart would "split". If she were told that all Nature was her to look at when she liked, "the news would strike her dead". All this would happen if she were to see Nature not with her physical eyes but with her mind's eye. The striking originality of the poem lies in the fact that it depicts the victory of the infinite over the finite or the triumph of the spiritual realization over the physical visualization. Thus selecting her own society in the form of self-imposed solitude, she adjusted herself well and felt :

> safer - guess - with just my soul
> Upon the window pane -
> Where other creatures put their eyes -
> Incautious - of the sun -[66]

Emily Dickinson is amazed at the vast panorama of the natural world and is curious and anxious to embrace as much as she can. Everywhere in the lap of Nature, something or other seems to fascinate and invite her :

There are signs to Nature's inns
Her invitation broad
For whomsoever famishing
To taste her mystic bread
These are the rites of Nature's house,
The hospitality
That opens with an equal width
To beggar or to bee.[67]

These poems again deviate from benign nature of Emersonion or wordsworthian tradition. Dickinson's predecessors conveniently ignored the destructiveness of the natural phenomena and even when they did not notice it, it was more or less with tacit approval for nature could not construct without destroying what was tainted or rotton. Emerson covered it further by having recourse to Hindi mythology to Brahma, one of whose attributes was destruction. That attitude however was on much higher and philosophical level.

Nature on the ostensible level remained a benevolent manifestation of a Being which watched the human drama with infinite sympathy, ready to guide man through the tangled web of his physical and ethical existence. Emily Dickinson cleared the cobweb of this confused pathetic fallacy. She saw man pittied against the terrifying brutal forces occasionally let loose by nature forces which in the blindness of their fury did not recognize the sanctity of man's existence, or his manifold interest. It was quite appropriate that she saw a thunderstorm as a monster, chuckling over the roof-tops; whistling in the air, shaking his fist gnashing his teeth, swinging her frenzied hair. Similarly elsewhere she writes:

The last summer is delight
Deterred by retrospect
Its ecstasy' revealed review.
Enchantment's syndicate.[68]

Inanimate Nature is also animate, like animal or person Dickinson not only animates the objects of nature but witnesses the process of growth and development in the world of nature also, which is parallel to the growth of the world of human beings :

> Growth of Man like growth of Nature
> Gravitates within
> Atmosphere and sun confirms it
> But it stirs alone ![69]

At times her reaction to beauty in nature sounds like the lyric cry of pain that had become a convention since the early nineteenth century.

> Beauty crowds me till I die
> Beauty mercy have on me
> But it I expire to-day
> Let it be is sight of thee -[70]

But this has less kinship with her romantic predecessors. She rejected the theological dogma, as she kept God and nature sharply differentiated even while she seized for her own purposes its aesthetic doctrines.

Beauty is Dickinson's name for the ecstasy with which we perceive that nature is the process of dying into immortality. She also kept man and nature separate, but as a sensitive poet, she was constantly drawn to speculate on its possible meanings for her; a subject that must be explored further in order to define how the poet makes use of Nature. Nature is a Haunted House but Art a House that tries to be haunted.

Emily Dickinson's keen observation of nature led her to believe that rain is accompanied by gentle breeze, tapping the door like visitor. Similarly, the wind is often accompanied by thunder-storm and tempest :

> An aweful tempest mashed the air
> The clouds were gaunt and few
> A black, as of a spectre's cloak
> Hid heaven and earth from view.[71]

But the impact of such an awful tempest on the world of nature is not a permanent feature; rather it is temporary and short-lived because

> The morning let, the birds arose
> The monster's faded eyes
> Turned slowly to his nature coast
> And peace was Paradise ![72]

Similarly, in another poem she conceives of the wind that does

> .... Working like a hand
> Whose fingers comb the sky
> Then quiver down, with tufts of tune
> Permitted gods and me.[73]

In spite of the various functions performed by the wind, Dickinson's mind is incessantly haunted by its monsterous picture destroying and affecting everything in the world of nature, unlike Shelley who puts his faith in it and seeks shelter and support of the wind !

> O lift me as a lead, a wave, a cloud,
> I fall upon the thorns of life, I bleed !

On the contrary, how anti-romantic Miss Dickinson seems when such poem as given below issues from her head and heart :

> The wind drew off
> Like hungry dogs
> Defeated of a bone
> Through fissures in
> Volcanic cloud
> The yellow lightning shown
> The trees held up
> Their mangled lenits
> Like animals in pain,
> When Nature falls
> Upon herself.[74]

Thus the poet has very dreadful associations with the wind, the storm causing chaos and confusion everywhere :

The Duties of the wind are few -
To cast the ships at sea,
Establish March
The Floods escort,
And usher Liberty.[75]

Sometimes Dickinson becomes amiable and cordial forgetting the hostility and cruelty shown by the wind and shows due hospitality to it as a guest"

The wind tapped like a tired man,
And like a host, "Come in."
I boldly answered : entered then
My residence within.[76]

Thus like Romantics, Emily Dickinson does not stick to some particular rigid dogma or theory, concerning the treatment of nature. Instead, from time to time her outlook to some objects of nature keeps changing. There is no hackneyed track for Emily Dickinson to follow. Her mind, like a good receptive, keeps inviting change after change. Thus she can enjoy or criticize the rare scenes of nature as she claims :

By my window have I for scenery

Thus Miss Dickinson's treatment of Nature in her poetry distinguished her from other Nature poets. While some of her early poems contain a conventional praise of Nature, as the gentlest mother", her mature attitude is absolutely different. For her, Nature remains mysterious and elusive and suffers a challenge to explore her hidden secrets. The more we scrutinize Nature's process, the more intricate and bewildering they become. To Dickinson, Nature exists as an alien, baffling force that defies full comprehension.

REFERENCES

1. Thomas H. Johnson. *The Complete Poems of Emily Dickinson*, (Delhi, Kalyani Publishers, 1910) Poem No. 441, p. 211.
2. William Wordsworth, Tintern Abbey, Lines No. 68-70.
3. *Ibid.*, Lines, 71-73.
4. *Ibid.*, Line, 92.

5. *Ibid.*, Lines, 94-97, 101 to 103.
6. *Ibid.*, Complete Poems, Poem No. 986, pp. 459-60.
7. *Ibid.*, Poem 790, p. 385.
8. William Wordsworth.
9. William Wordsworth, *Ode to Immortality*, Stanza XI, lines 16-17.
10. Johnson, *Complete Poems*, Poem No. 101, p. 49.
11. *Ibid.*, Poem No. 304, p. 143.
12. *Ibid.*, Poem No. 198, p. 93.
13. Johnson, *Complete Poems*, Poem No. 232, p. 106.
14. *Ibid.*
15. *Ibid.*, Poem 1397, pp. 598-599.
16. Johnson, *Complete Poems*, Poem No. 94, p. 47.
17. *Ibid.*, Poem No. 318, p. 150.
18. *Ibid.*, Poem No. 228, p. 104.
19. *Ibid.*, Poem No. 191, p. 90.
20. *Ibid.*
21. *Ibid.*, Poem No. 824, p. 400.
22. *Ibid.*, Poem No. 1593, pp. 659-660.
23. *Ibid.*, Poem No. 404, p. 192.
24. Ibid., Poem No. 757, p. 371.
25. *Ibid.*, Poem No. 140, p. 65.
26. *Ibid.*, Poem No. 74, p. 38.
27. *Ibid.*
28. *Ibid.*, Poem No. 844, p. 407.
29. *Ibid.*, Poem No. 812, p. 395.
30. *Ibid.*
31. *Ibid.*, Poem No. 140, p. 65.
32. *Ibid.*, Poem No. 99, p. 49.
33. *Ibid.*, Poem No. 342, p. 162.
34. *Ibid.*
35. *Ibid.*, Poem No. 17, p. 14.
36. *Ibid.*, Poem No. 1320, pp. 572-573.
37. *Ibid.*, Poem No. 133, pp. 62-63.
38. *Ibid.*, Poem No. 619, p. 305.

39. Martha Dickinson Bianchi and Alfred Lecte Hampson (eds) Poems by Emily Dickinson. Introduction by Alfred Lecte Hampson (Boston: Little Brown and Company 1952), Poem - XIII, p. 237.
40. Johnson, *Complete Poems*, Poem No. 1170, p. 520-521.
41. *Ibid.*, Poem No. 668, p. 332.
42. Johnson, *Complete Poems*, Poem No. 1333, p. 577.
43. *Ibid.*, Poem No. 1079, p. 489.
44. Johnson, *Complete Poems*, Poem No. 575, p. 280.
45. *Ibid.*, Poem No. 516, p. 252.
46. *Ibid.*, Poem No. 766, p. 375.
47. *Ibid.*, Poem No. 1400, pp. 599-600.
48. *Ibid.*, Poem No. 1619, pp. 666-667.
49. *Ibid.*, Poem No. 333, p. 157.
50. *Ibid.*, Poem No. 1510, p. 634.
51. *Ibid.*, Poem No. 364, pp. 172-173.
52. *Ibid.*, Poem No. 348, pp. 165-166.
53. *Ibid.*, Poem No. 1400, pp. 599-600.
54. *Ibid.*
55. *Ibid.*, Poem No. 1624, pp. 667-668.
56. *Ibid.*, Poem No. 74, pp. 38-39.
57. *Ibid.*, Poem No. 986, pp. 459-460.
58. *Ibid.*, Poem No. 1575, p. 653.
59. *Ibid.*, Poem No. 1298, pp. 565-566.
60. *Ibid.*, Poem No. 328, p. 156.
61. *Ibid.*, Poem No. 1463, p. 619.
62. *Ibid.*, Poem No. 1068, p. 485.
63. *Ibid.*, Poem No. 794, p. 389.
64. *Ibid.*, Poem No. 436, pp. 209-210.
65. *Ibid.*, Poem No. 327, p. 155.
66. *Ibid.*
67. *Op. cit.*, Poem No. 1077, pp. 488-489.
68. Johnson, Poem No. 1353, p. 584.
69. *Ibid.*, Poem No. 750, p. 367.
70. *Ibid.*, Poem No. 1654, pp. 676-677.
71. *Ibid.*, Poem No. 198, pp. 93-94.

72. *Ibid.*
73. *Op. cit.*
74. Johnson, *Complete Poems*, Poem No. 1694, p. 691.
75. *Ibid.*, Poem No. 1137, p. 510.
76. *Op. cit.*, Poem No. 436, p. 209.

LOVE POEMS

3

> Oh the Earth was made for lovers,
>
> \- - - - - -
>
> God hath made nothing single but thee in His world so fair[1]

Emily Dickinson, being an introvert type of personality, never wished her romance to be probed. This plea became irrelevant the moment her status as a poet was made evident. If her family had wished to protect her private life from scrutiny, there was only one way to do it, a way clearly marked at for them by her own life long refusal to publish her poems. They chose instead to publish, and, in doing so, they gave a rightful place to Emily in the company of Wordsworth, Keats and Browning.

Apart from the poems written on the theme of Nature, she wrote more than a hundred poems on the theme of love. An overwhelming majority of them were written during the years 1861-1863. But with the passage of time, she altogether banished love from her poetry. Except for the years of adolescenthood, she lived in austere seclusion, declining in later years to meet even intimate friends. These starting facts about her lead us to inevitable question: where did she get the experience to write these love poems? Critics and biographers have difference of opinion and present the life of Emily Dickinson as unconvincing mystery and an unresolved controversy.

As her poems were printed posthumously, and as they now stand, these lyrics are presented in no intelligible order. The sequence of her love poems is broken into scattered fragments and its design is lost.

In various poems, Emily Dickinson has described a visit to the ocean which never took place and her own death-bed sensations and her feelings as she rested in the grave. Were her love poems like these figments of the imagination or were they reports in verse of what she had actually experienced ? The question is important in forming a second estimate of Emily Dickinson's personality and her quality as a writer. She was the subject of irresponsible gossip during her life-time. We can hardly blame the "outsiders" as many a hot or quaint tale emanated from a source very close to the poet herself. She writes that her life has been too simple and stern to embarrass any.

Everyone connected with Amherst between 1850-1880, was vaguely aware of the mysterious love affairs attributed to Dickinson's peculiar daughter, though these rumours were not openly repeated.

All the legends are reducible to two basic types. The first has to do with an early attachment with an eligible young man. Benjamine Fraklin Newton, who stirred in her an undoubted intellectual independence and stimulated her aesthetic sensibility. But Emily's father discouraged her and restricted her from going ahead in this love-affair, on the ground that the suitor's prospects were not satisfactory and sufficiently hopeful. Gossip specifies a lover's meeting in the garden interrupted by lantern light, a sterm father ordering the youngman off the premises, defiant Emily, promising never to leave her home until her love could claim her and to wear nothing but white for his sake, and a broken-hearted love dying after a few years of agonized separation. His premature death prevented her friendship from developing into love. Therefore it is fairly safe to presume that her relationship with him was that of a devoted and a sympathetic teacher. This fact is proved by the letter in which she always refers to him as "friend", "tutor" and "preceptor". She wrote no poem to commemorate her friendship with Newton. But by that time she had fallen in love with Rev. Charles Wadsworth, who held the same belief as her father and it was quite plausible that he preached on a subject dear to her and left an abiding impression on her highly sensitive mind.

But Dickinson's love for Wadsworth was unique and cannot be described as "love-affair". If love it was, it was a hopeless and one-sided love which did not experience fulfillment even in an embrace. After her death, the rough drafts of these love-letters were found, which were never sent to him. Wadsworth was married and had four children. She must have known that it would be highly indiscreet to unburden the agonizing secret of her heart.

No doubt, Dickinson's love for Wadsworth deepened her sympathy and stimulated her creative activity yet love affairs do not always make a poet. And therefore this is wrong to believe that she would not have been a poet without this experience. She was a poet before she fell in love but considering the amazing large number of poems, she composed after 1860. One cannot feel to notice the sudden blossoming of her genius as a poet. Besides, all her love poems belong to this period. It may be a strange co-incidence but her creative impulse came to her as a tide and receded soon after the crisis in her heart had subsided to a life-long yearning. Hence she decided to suffer in silence and her love for Wadsworth remained a closely guarded secret all her life.

Emily Dickinson was an eager school-girl with a craving for vital knowledge that no formal institution could satisfy. Books were of course a frugal chariot for the exploring soul, but better than books was intercourse with minds that she regarded as superior to her own. She felt thirst for intellectual and spiritual guidance. It was the master passion of her life. Her words make it clear that at least two men had profoundly influenced her mind. One was the friend of her girlhood who taught her "Immortality". The other was the "One more" who in leaving the land had left her without a master. Both were now lost to her. The identification of these two friends give us the key to the crisis of Emily's life.

In 1854, Emily wrote to Reverend Edward Hale, about the spiritual state of her mind for a man who had been dear to her:

> I think Sir, you were the Postor of Mr. B.F. Newton who died and I have often hoped to know if his last

> hours were cheerful, and if he was willing to die .... You may think my desire strange, Sir, but the Dead was dear to me, and I would like to know that he sleeps peacefully ...., Mr. Newton become to a gentle, yet grave preceptor, teaching me what to read, what authors to admire, what was most ground or beautiful in nature, and that sublime lesson, a faith in things unseen, and in a life again nobler and much more blessed .... Please, Sir, tell me if he was willing to die and if you think him at Home, I should love as much to know certainly that he was to-day in heaven.[2]

The above words of Emily throb with a scarcely restrained emotion. She had reason to be grateful to Ben Newton for he had put her in touch with new and stimulating currents of thought beyond the range of orthodox upbringing. He had told her that she had the power to be a poet and had praised her early verses in terms that she never forgot. The lonely, rigid domestic life of Emily Dickinson breathed fresh air with the arrival of Newton. Thus Bengamin Newton provided even more exciting and rich diet to the anxious and curious heart of young Emily. With Ben Newton's help. Emily first surveyed a wider horizon than her father's house could show her and sent her mind adventuring in the exciting world of ideas that the new visions disclosed. There is direct evidence also that Newton discovered her faculty for poetic composition, confirmed it by his praise of her early poems, gave her confidence in her powers and urged her to dedicate all her energies to the cultivation of her great gift.

There is nothing to show that Emily Dickinson, though she loved Newton as an elder brother, even considered him as a possible husband. He was always her tutor. Indeed she missed him greatly. Her loneliness and depression are discernible in her letters in spite of a gallant attempt to maintain a playful tone. She wrote to Abiah of this event as her "first affliction" but some phrases in the letter sound as though she had another sorrow in mind, though its nature is somewhat obscure. She writes:

"I am selfish too, because I am feeling lonely, some of my friends are gone, and some of my friends are sleeping, the churchyard sleep .... I will try not to say any more-my rebellious thoughts are many and the friend I love and trust in has much now to forgive". Thus the untimely death of Newton shocked Emily, yet she calmly suffered in silence the void left by Benjamine Newton -

The news of Wadsworth's acceptance of a call to the calvary church was received by Emily with a sense of crisis and it is from this time onwards that she mentions calvary in her love poems. In 1862 alone this name appears in nine poems. In 1863, she began her incomplete poems in rough draft with the moving lines :

Where thou art - that is Home
Cashmere or Calvary the same.[3]

It is sometimes after this event that she adopted her "white election" and began to dress in immaculate white and withdrew from life to concentrate on her poetry. This withdrawl is often misinterpreted as renunciation. But the fact is that Emily had nothing to renounce.

It is to Emily's credit that even after her disappointment, she was aware of her talent as a poet. She gathered her forces for writing poetry with singleminded devotion. It was a conscious and deliberate choice and any sympathy for her life long solitude would be misplaced. If she was a loneliness she shared with all great artists of the world; still she continued to mourn for him and struggled to comprehend the inexorable fate that consigned golden lads like Newton and Humphrey to dust. She returned to her writing with a deeper instruction, and also speaks freely of the "two she lost." A few other allusions in her poetry were prompted by recollections of her earliest friend:

A book I have a friend gave
Whose pencil, here and there
Had notched, the place that pleased him-
At rest his fingers are
Now when I read, I read not
For interrupting tears

Obliterate the etchings
Too costly for repairs.[4]

She recalls everything connected with the life of her dead friend. When she picks up the books presented by her dead-friend, her heart is filled with extreme sorrow. She is afraid that the falling of tears might remove the etchings which are so costly now and which she wants to preserve as her valuable treasure.

After her grieving was softened by Time's consummate plush, Dickinson returned to the theme of the "lost jewel" and rewrote it to suit her later taste. She wrote to honour her friend by lavishing upon him all the gorgeousness and she had learned the value of severe economy:

I held a jewel in my fingers
And went to sleep
The day was warm, winds were prosy
I said, "I will keep,"
I woke and child my honest fingers
The gem was gone
And now an amethyst remembrance
Is all I own.[5]

Apart from Benjamin Newton and Wadsworth, Mr. Lord also left an indelible mark on the sensitive mind of Emily Dickinson. In fact, Emily had known Mr. Lord all her life. He entered Amherst College before she was born and graduated when she was not yet two years old. Although much younger than Mr. Dickinson, he became as She said, "my father's closest friend," We must recognize the fact that whereas she had always honoured Judge Lord as her father's best friend, after his death, she seems to have felt toward him a veneration, a primitive kind of awe.

There was soon a further excuse for Emily's increasing "cowardice of strangers". In June 1875, a year from the evening father died, her mother was paralysed "I have no Father and scarcely a Mother" she wrote to Higginson, Mrs. Dickinson was beginning to regain the ability to walk about the house when in time 1878, she broke her lip. After that she was helpless and not of power to lift her head for a glass of water. Emily's time was devoted to attending to her mother's dear little wants until in November 1882 she died.

On Emily's forty seventh birth day, Judge Lord received a paralyzing blow. His wife - a woman of power as well as of unusual beauty - died on December 10, 1877; Emily sprang to comfort him. It was her custom to minister her friends in the time of bereavements. Later, on July 16, 1878, Samuel Bowels, died, Dr. Wadsworth on April 7, 1882, and her mother on November 10, 1882.

As related by her niece, the legend of Emily's withdrawal from the world because of a youthful disappointment in love has been accepted as the truth. The legend arose during Emily's life-time because Amherst gossips could not understand either her secluded life or the cryptic little messages in verse and in prose, which she sent about to her neighbours. She certainly was 'queer' so it was whispered that she sought seclusion because of a hopeless love for a married man. This was not only plausible but also the most accepted explanation of her conduct.

The important thing to note is that the attachment between Judge Lord and Emily was real and that it was mutual. It was not romantic fantasy on her part. Emily did not write these letters just to relieve her feelings, she wrote them for Lord Judge to read.

With the above background of Emily's life, it to not easy to give a clear-cut explanation of the workings of the mind and heart of Emily Dickinson. In fact, her heart and head is full of complexities which puzzle our mind incessantly. To fall in love with a married man is one thing; to cherish a love which is not even mutual is altogether a different matter. The desire to love and to be loved, is universal enough but to love without the desire to be loved is a unique case, and puzzles the mind of a the writers. If Freudian theories are pressed into service for explanation, it may appear neurotic. Neurosis, in psycho-analytical terminology, is a convenient handle to explain everything which does not conform to the conventional pattern.

Emily never sought fulfilment of her love. In one poem she writes :

> I'd rather recollect a setting
> Than own a rising sun.[6]

Thus Emily Dickinson consciously endeavoured to preserve the freshness of her dream rather than see the reality. What she needed in life was a preceptor and a muse whom she could adore with physical passion in her imagination. In fact, it is in woman's nature that the memory of longing survives the more fugitive memory of fulfilment. She shows her belief in the laws of opposition. According to her experiences of life, she concludes that defeat is superior to victory, since an achieved victory soon loses its value and worth. The idea of compensation or the superiority of defeat over victory is reflected in quite a number of poems of Emily. This is very significant aspect of her poetry as it reveals one of the paradoxes of Emily's life. She mastered life by rejecting it; What she lacked in social life, she gained in secluded life. The idea of juxtaposition, paradox plays a predominant role in her poetry:

> Success is counted sweetest
> By those who never succeed
> To comprehend a nectar
> Requires sorest need.[7]

Here Emily expresses the idea of compensation; the idea that every evil confers some balancing good, that through bitterness we are able to appreciate the sweet that "water is taught by thirst". The defeated and dying soldier in the above poem is compensated by a greater awareness of the meaning of victory or frustration over satisfaction. For the dying soldier, the material loss leads spiritual gain, which is more valuable, precious and everlasting. Thus the definition of victory is better comprehended by the defeated, dying ear. Again she writes.

> Undue significance a starving man attaches
> To food-
> Far off-He-sighs-and therefore - Hopeless-
> And therefore - Good-[8]

Similarly in the same mood she writes another poem beginning with "My portion is defeat to-day..." which she ends in the following manner:

How different victory to him
Who has it, and the one
Who to have had it would have been
Contenteder to die.[9]

Thus, the above extracts from her poems suggest that a starving man's vision of food or a dying man's vision of victory are but wishfulfilment. But the experience of Emily's life taught her that food, victory or love or any other thing is best comprehended by the eye of desire from the vantage of privation.

Emily Dickinson did not achieve what she deserved. The deprivation and love and literary recognition at times led her to realize that she lacked spiritual community but she compensated for all the losses and began her career with normal appetite for recognition.

Emily never accepted Emerson's belief in the harmonious correspondence of man and Nature. She viewed man as an estranged, beleaguered creature, who is put under continual stress without any certainty, that his pain will merit salvation. A desire best defines a thing. Anticipation and search are all important. Desire allows the intellect and the imagination to comprehend nectar, something precious given only to gods in the heaven. Similarly she writes-

Love is done when Love's begun
Sages say,[10]

Another example conveying the same idea :

Experience is the Angled Road
Preferred against the Mind
By - paradox - the Mind itself-
Presuming it to lead.[11]

Thus she ratioinalized loss into gain, relishing even the bitterness of life.

Thus the poems mentioned above, deal with the laws of compensation and interrelation of pain and pleasure, ecstasy and despair. She viewed both sides of an experience and unhindered by the dogma or traditional concepts, accepted life as it occurred. Sometimes she claimed that anticipation surpassed attainment and that pain alone endured while happiness was denied. Emily believed as an artist that her response to experience could best be realized in the rarefied private world of her own where human encounters did not blunt the edge of her sensitive soul:

> The soul's superior instants
> Occur to Her - alone -
> When friend - and Earth's occasion
> Have infinite withdrawn-[12]

In another poem she writes :

> The soul that hath a guest
> Doth seldom go abroad -
> Diviner crowd at home -
> Obliterate the need.

To a life of humdrum routine, she preferred the life in the world of her imagination where she could love with greater fullness and intensity.

> The soul selects her own society
> Then shuts the Door-[13]

In the above poem also she repeats the same idea. This poem has some relation to her choice of a life of solitude, made about this time, preferring her own circle and closing the door on the general world, as the opening lines of the poem suggest. But the 'select society' is specifically limited to the chosen "one" of the third stanza. A surface reading of the poem categorizes it into a simple love poem and the central stanza supports the view for the "pausing chariots" and the "kneeling emperor", suggest future suitors being rejected because of the "chosen one" rather than the temptations of society that might distract her from her art. On the other hand, "One" may be God finally there is the hint of nunnery, where she waits for God alone, the king of heaven.

Nothing can be said for certain that this chosen "One" is earthly lover or heavenly. But this much is certain that to all others she turns a heart of stone that makes her choice final.

The largest group of her love poems, indicating her devotion and loyalty remained uncommunicated to the object of her love: they occur in their varying degree for her own relief and satisfaction.

In one of her early poems Emily adopts the impersonal third person to describe what apparently is her own nervous confusion at meeting her lover face to face.

> The Rose did caper on her cheek-
> Her Boddice rose and fell.[14]

Her speech staggers like drunken men and her fingers fumble at her needle. Such intensity of emotion is the prerogative of a pure heart at its first encounter with love.

In another poem Emily cherishes the hope of her complete identification with her lover in all humility:

> Forever of His fate to taste-
> In grief - the largest past -
> If joy - to put my piece away
> For that beloved heart[15]

Again she repeats the idea in another poem where she anxiously waits for the moment when she would avail a chance to see the face of her lover. She is absorbed in deep thoughts:

> What would I give to see his face ?
> I'd give - I'd give my life - of course -
> But that is not enough
> Stop just a minute - let me think !
> I'd give my biggest bobolink ![16]

Emily is willing to give her life and all that is precious to her to see his face" and then jokingly asks :

> Now - have I bought it -
> 'Shylock"? Say !
> Sign me the bond.[17]

As the drop of water loses its identity in the sea, she would lose her in him. She would carry his face with her when she goes "out of time" :

The face I carry with me - last -
When I go out of time -
To take my Rank -by- in the West -
That face - will just be thine -[18]

Walls would be no barrier to her even if the "Universe" was one solid rock, she would "tunnel" at "his silver call: for the recompense to look in his eyes"

I had not minded - walls
Were universe - one Rock -
And far I heard his silver call
The other side the Block -[19]

As the moon leads the sea like a docile boy, She wishes to be guided by "the Amber Hand" She loved him as Jesus loved men.

That He - loved Men -
As I - love thee[20]

His love come to her like fire and made "her house" glow in its radiant light; it was like the sunrise in the sky.

Impanelled from no summer brief -
With limit of decay -
'T was Noon - without the News of Night
Nay, Nature it was Day,[21]

The love poems of Emily Dickinson, cover a vast variety of moods and temperament. Although she possesses a strong desire to see his face, yet her failure to see her sovereign's face on the earth inspires her to get her wish fulfilled in the life hereafter in the kingdom of heaven, but there she finds no entry:

Why-do they shut me out of Heaven ?
Did I sing - too loud ?
But - I can say a little "Minor"
Timid as a Bird !
Wouldn't the Angls by me -
Just - once - more -

Just - see - if I troubled them -
But don't - shut the door ![22]

Sometimes in a movement of intense longing, Emily says that she would be contented it, like a stranger in "an ungracious country, he paused at her door for a short while and if she was permitted to be the housewife in the cottage he lived.

.... The Tenant of the Narrow Cottage, Wert thou -
Permit to be
The Housewife in thy low attendance
contendeth Me.[23]

There are the ever changing shades of Emily's devoted love as she writes about it. The picture that emerges through these poems is that of a shy, modest and self-effacing girl, who was willing to sacrifice all that she had on the altar of love and who needed only a little sunshine to make her happy. But fate had ordained otherwise.

The first poem on the theme of love was written in 1862 after Wadsworth had left for San Francisco. Emily Dickinson thought the Nature would be different after the crisis and sympathise with the "Queen of Calvary" as she called herself. But everything was as usual, except herself who alone felt the loss:

It makes no difference abroad -
The seasons - fit - the same -
The Morning blossom into Noons -
And split their pods of Flame -[24]

She had hoped that robin, the daffodils, the grass, the bees would not come with summer but—

They're here, though not a creature failed
No blossom, stayed away.
In gentle deference to me-
The queen of calvary -[25]

In her despair, Emily asks the rose not to scatter its colour and sweetness as she has lost the capacity to enjoy them; she grieves at the prospect and wonders what she would do when the roses blossom and birds fly in the maple tree, or—

Oh, when the squirrel fills His pockets
And the Berries stare
How can I bear their jocund Faces
Thou From there, so far ?[26]

Thus Nature's indifference to her sufferings leads her to utter disappointment and dejecton. Realizing that the gulf which separates them cannot be bridged, Emily envies those who have physical proximity to him. She envies the sea and the "spokes of wheels of chariots" on which he rides and those who "gaze" on his journey :

I envy Light - that wakes Him -
And Bells - that boldly ring
To tell Him it is Noon, abroad -[27]

She comments on the permanence of her love she adjusted her being, carved her being upon it, then exiled herself in the East.

He found my Being - set it up -
Adjusted it to place -
Then carved his name - upon it -
And bade it to the East.[28]

To die for him was easier than to live unhappily without him, which includes dying manifold without the respite granted to the dead—

Too scanty 'twas to die for you
- - - - -
The Dying is a trifle, past,
But living, this include
The dying multifold - without
The Respite to be dead.[29]

Again, the fulfilment of their love was interject of God and their separation was preordained.

Ended, ere it begun -
- - - - - -
That it was not and privilege
The interdict of God -[30]

In such a hopeless situation, the only hope that was left to Emily was that she would achieve after her death what she had failed to accomplish in life. Such a hope is common enough and has become almost a human weakness, which all the religions of the world have explained in promising the bounties of God, denied to man in wordly existence. One wonders how the allurements of the next world have lightened the burden of many a man and woman and they have borme cheerfully the misery of this world in the hope of getting a recompense in the next world. Emily Dickinson was no exception. She cautiously mentions the possibility of her achieving "victory" in one of her poems. She struggles hard to cross the barriers in the path of love and finds her horizons blocked'.

They strive — and yet delay
They perish — Do we die
Or is this Death's -Experiment -
Reserved - in Victory ?[31]

She even anticipates how she would feel when she meets him after this life. In two of her love poems, termed as "bridal poems", she expresses her conviction that after a long parting she would meet him", before the judgement seat of God," where she would be eternally united with him. Emily thinks of true, grave as the little cottage where like a bride, she keeps "the Parlor ready "lays 'marble tea' for him and wants to be united in everlasting life.

The grave my little cottage is
Where "Keeping house" for thee
I make my parlor orderly
And lay the marble tea.
- - - - -
Till everlasting life unite
In strong society.[32]

Her deep sorrow in love gave her the necessary insight to analyse pain :

Pain-has an element of Blank -
It cannot recollect
When it begun -[33]

Similarly one is shocked after a tragic crisis and the soul becomes paralysed, without being able to remember anything.

After great pain, a formal feeling comes -[34]

There is a close affinity between the love poems of Emily Dickinson and John Donne. The latter has lavishly used metaphysical conceits which give precision and pointedness to his utterance. Although Emily did not consciously employ this artifice in her poetry, there are occasional flashes of great beauty. In one of her poems, She contrasts the merits of her lover with her own unworthiness. Again in a metaphysical conceit, Emily compares her life to a loaded gun, filled with emotional force and sensitivity but standing forsaken in a pawn-shop, waiting for redemption. Thus the central conceit of a loaded gun signifies a potential, inert force, one with explosive power which can only be released by another. The concept of the active male hunter possessing the passive woman guides the whole poem.

My life had stood - a Loaded gun -
In corners - till a Day
The owner passed - identified -
And carried me away-[35]

But the concluding lines of the poem hint at the death which will grant them a chance for spiritual salvation and immortality. His domination has so exhausted her spirit that she is lifeless and inert without his love.

In two of her poems, Emily Dickinson has employed sexual imagery. She feels that a stormly wild night will become a luxury if she were with him for 'a heart in part'.

Wild Nights - Wild Night !
Were I with thee
Wild Nights Should be
Our Luxury ![36]

If he is with her, there is no need of sailor's compass or chart and the howling winds outside can do no harm.

Rowing in Eden -
Ah the Sea !

Might I but moor - Tonight -
In thee ![37]

Love taught Emily Dickinson patience and fortitude, which gave a new dimension of her personality. It is through the experience of love that she matured and explored within herself the "undiscovered continent". The voyage of discovery gave a philosophical depth to her thinking and enriched her vision of life.

Emily's approach to love varies from time to time. No doubt, sometimes she expressed earthly or profane love. But such an interpretation is fairly damaged at times when we come across such lines as :

I tend my flowers for thee -
Bright Absentee ![38]

Here she is talking metamorphically and the "flowers" are her own accomplishments which she prunes and improves upon in preparation for the day when she may meet her "absentee" whose image is still clear and bright in her imagination, in spite of the lapse of time.

That Love is all there is
Is all we know of Love.[39]

In the above lines Emily tells that the all pervading force of love inheres in all objects of this universe and gives relevance and meaning to the cosmic order. She also goes a step further and identifies love with the Diety:

Unable are the loved to die
For love is Immortality
Nay, it is Diety[40]

Thus according to Emily Diskinson, Love merges with Deity and takes the shape by divinity and becomes immortal. She has even thought of Lord Christ as her divine lover and in some of her bridal poems, she has described her marriage with the Saviour. In Christian tradition, the nuns are known as the brides-of-Lamb and she thought of herself as the bride of Christ. Her habit of dressing herself in immaculate white bridal dress from the age of thirty till her death was perhaps motivated by the same desire.

In Hindu tradition, the highest form of worship for a woman is to regard the Lord as her husband. This attitude was popularized by the Indian saint-poet Mira Bai who always sang of Lord Krishna as her husband.

Since her early childhood, Mira deemed herself to be the bride of the Lord and sang and danced with complete self-surrender. Even after her marriage with Rana of Udaipur, she refused to accept anybody else as her husband. The agitated Rana sent her a poisoned cup of drink but the poison had no effect on her; rather she enjoyed it like nectar :

> The Rana sent the poisoned cup
> But the living Mira danced to the Lord

There is a close resemblance between the bridal songs of Emily Dickinson and the devotional songs of Mira Bai. In some of her bridal poems. Emily thought of the entire ceremony of marriage in purely temporal terms:

> A wife - at Daybreak I shall be -
> Sunrise - Hast thou a Flag for me ?
> At Midnight, I am but a Maid,
> How short it takes to make it Bride-
> Then - Midnight, I have passed from thee
> Unte the East, and Victory[41]

After that Emily bids goodnight to the night as she hears the bustles of angels in the hall and as her future bridegroom climbs the stairs to take her to the marriage ceremony. The midnight refers to the periods of her spiritual darkness of worldly existence and the morning represents her awakening from the midnight of temporal life and her transfer to the celestial life after death. Responding to the call she says :

> Eternity, I'm coming - Sir,
> Saviour - I've seen the face - before![42]

In the above lines, she is referring to the eternal life after death when, married to the saviour, she will be merged with eternity.

Emily always thought of divine marriage as love's baptism. or a second baptism.

I'm ceded - I've stopped being Their's
The name they dropped upon my face.[43]

She expresses the accomplishment of her marriage with Christ and this new name and status, and now she no more belongs to her parents. She was baptized in her infancy without her choice. But now with the second baptism or marriage with Lord Christ, the "Supreme name" is a deliberate choice. Earlier at the time of her first baptism, she was half conscious of her status and was brought to the ceremony "crowning". But at the time of her second baptism, she is fully conscious of the dignity to be conferred upon her :

Baptised, before without the choice
But this time, consciously, of grace -
Unto supreme name -
- - - -
With will to chose, or to reject -
And I choose just a crown -"[44]

There is yet another explicit example of her celestial marriage in another poem :

Give in Marriage unto Thee
Oh then celestial Host -
Bride of the Father and the Son
Bride of the Holy Ghost[45]

The celestial marriage conquers death and "the keeper of this Ring" will no longer be subject to spiritual mortality, even though physical death may come to her as to others.

The analysis of the bridal poems of Emily Dickinson shows her absolute dedication to Lord Christ and surrender of the self to Him. In one of her poems, she presents a dialogue between Jesus and herself in most familiar terms, used only by lovers :

Unto Me ? I do not know you -
Where may be your House ?
I am Jesus - Late of Judea
Now - of Paradise -[46]

At the call of the Lord, she bluntly replies that she does not know Him. On being told who He is, she readily agrees to accompany Him but again asks if he has conveyance to carry her, on being assured that His arms are enough to carry her. She again feigns ignorance and offers lame excuses"

> I am spotted - "I am Pardon"
> I am small - The Least
> Is esteemed in Heaven the Chiefest -
> Occupy my House -[47]

She is speaking of her spiritual experience but the imagery is chosen from profane love.

Emily returns to the same coquettish delay of her surrender to Jesus in another poem :

> Just so - Jesus - raps -
> He - doesn't weary -
> \- - - - -
> Then - on divinest tiptoe - standing -
> Might He but sky the lady's soul-[48]

"The lady's soul" is the poet's own soul in hiding when Jesus knocks at her door, first at the bell, then at the knocker. He stands on his Divinest tiptoe waiting for her, creating a fear in her that he may spy her soul hiding because of the awareness of her imperfections. The poet hopes that when he retires to his chamber, it will be her turn to go to him and wait for him at his door, but for that, there is ample time. Patient till such moment arrives, she has only to knock at her own heart which is thrilled at the prospect of meeting Jesus.

The same mood of cheerfulness and self-assurance does not prevail in all her love - poems. In one of her poems, Emily describes the agony of her soul, boarding on despair, at her inability to find Jesus. The only course left to her is to pray to him. She holds the conviction that if the arms of Jesus can set at rest the earthquake or the 'maelstrom', they not set at rest the turbulence of her soul? The answer is in the affirmative, but she is further subjected to depression and agony:

> At least - to pray - is left - is left -
> Oh Jesus - in the Air -
> I know not which thy chamber is -

I'm knocking - everywhere -
Thou settest Earthquake in the south -
And Maelstrom in the sea -
Say, Jesus Christ, of Nazareth -
Heart thou no Arms for Me?[49]

Again the imagery in this love poem is taken from the earthly love. The frantic beloved, not knowing the exact chamber of her Lord, is knocking everywhere. No doubt, the above poem is a cry of despair. It is a record of mind overwhelmed by an emotion from which it cannot detach itself.

In another poem, a sense of perspective begins to appear :

Of course I prayed -
And did God ease ?
And eased as much
As on the air
A Bird - had stamped her foot -
And cried "give Me".[50]

Here the poetic expression rises as the emotion is brought under control. The poetess is able to look back at her despair and has time to recollect herself and to estimate results and finally it becomes the occasion of completely impersonal reflection in "Prayer is the little implement."

(Men) fling their speech
By means of it in God's ear:
If then he bear
This sums the apparatus
Comprised in prayer[51]

The above poem on prayer, clearly rises out of an emotional crisis, though the note of crisis is not specified. It refers to the main crisis of her life. A number of Emily Dickinson's love poems contain no hint of pain or loss and are so far from sharing the agonized mood of "At least to pray" is left, that it is natural to suppose that many of them were written before she had undergone the shipwreck of her hope.

Divine love was as much Emily Dickinson's concern as earthly love and this grants originality to her love poems.

REFERENCES

1. Thomas H. Johnson, *The Complete Poems of Emily Dickinson*, (Delhi, Kalyani Publisher, Poem No. 1), p. 3.
2. G.F. Whicher, *This was A Poet: A Critical Biography of Emily Dickinson*. (New York, 1938), pp. 53-54.
3. Johnson, *The Complete Poems*, Poem No. 725, pp. 355-356.
4. *Ibid.*, Poem No. 360, pp. 170-171.
5. *Op. cit.*, Poem No. 245, p. 112.
6. Johnson, *The Complete Poems*, Poem No. 1349, p. 583.
7. *Ibid.*, Poem No. 67, p. 35.
8. *Op. cit.*, Poem No. 67, p. 35.
9. Johnson, *The Complete Poems*, Poem No. 638, p. 316.
10. *Ibid.*, Poem No. 1485, p. 627.
11. *Op. cit.*, Poem No. 910, p. 430.
12. *Ibid.*, Poem No. 306, p. 144.
13. *Op. cit.*, Poem No. 303, p. 143.
14. *Ibid.*, Poem No. 208, p. 97.
15. Johnson, *The Complete Poems*, Poem No. 246, p. 112.
16. *Op. cit.*, Poem No. 247, p. 113.
17. *Idem.*
18. *Op. cit.*, Poem No. 336, p. 159.
19. *Ibid.*, Poem No. 398, p. 189.
20. Johnson, *The Complete Poems*, Poem No. 456, p. 219.
21. *Ibid.*, Poem No. 638, p. 316.
22. *Ibid.*, Poem No. 248, pp. 113-114.
23. *Ibid.*, Poem No. 961, pp. 449-450.
24. *Ibid.*, Poem No. 620, p. 306.
25. *Op. cit.*, Poem No. 348, p. 165.
26. *Op. cit.*, Poem No. 956, p. 447.
27. Johnson, *The Complete Poems*, Poem 498, p. 241.
28. *Ibid.*, Poem No. 603, p. 296.
29. *Ibid.*, Poem No. 1013, p. 468.
30. *Ibid.*, Poem No. 1088, p. 493.
31. *Ibid.*, Poem No. 550, p. 268.
32. *Ibid.*, Poem No. 1743, p. 706.
33. *Ibid.*, Poem No. 650, p. 323.

34. *Ibid.*, Poem No. 341, p. 162.
35. *Ibid.*, Poem No. 754, p. 369.
36. *Ibid.*, Poem No. 249, p. 114.
37. *Idem.*
38. *Ibid.*, Poem No. 339, pp. 160-161.
39. *Ibid.*, Poem No. 1765, p. 714.
40. *Ibid.*, Poem No. 809, p. 394.
41. *Ibid.*, Poem No. 461, p. 222.
42. *Idem.*
43. *Op. cit.*, Poem, 508, p. 247.
44. *Idem.*
45. *Op. cit.*, Poem No. 817, p. 397.
46. Johnson, *The Complete Poems*, Poem No. 964, p. 451.
47. *Idem.*
48. *Ibid.*, Poem No. 317, p. 149.
49. *Ibid.*, Poem No 502, pp. 243-244.
50. *Op. cit.*, Poem No. 376, pp. 179-180.
51. *Ibid.*, Poem No. 437, p. 210.

PRE-OCCUPATION WITH DEATH

4

He fought like those who've nought to lose:

... ...
Invited Death with bold attempt
But Death was coy of him
As other men were coy of Death !
To him, to live was doom.[1]

Death, "that lonesome glory", is one of the perennial themes of poetry. In English Literature, there is the graveyard school of poetry, where death forms the focal point of all the observations on the illusionary nature of human existence and its equally ephemeral vanities. Fear of death is natural enough for it bears testimony to the universal love of life, and death is the most formidable adversary of love.

In English and American poetry, before Emily Dickinson, and even in recent years, the concern of the poet has been with emotions, not necessarily fear, caused by death as in the great elegies of the nineteenth century. There has been no attempt to find the meaning of death or to define the mystery which has be wildered human understanding."

Life is what we make it
Death we do not know
Christ's acquaintance with him.
Justifies Him, though
\- - - - -
His sure feet proceeding
Tender Pioneer -
Base must be the cowards
Dare not venture now.[2]

Although mystery pervades regarding the conception of death, yet Christ's acquaintance with Death justifies its reality. In another poem Emily Dickinson writes :

> All but death can be Adjusted
> Dynasties repaired -
> Systems - settled in their sockets
> Citadels - dissolved
> Death unto itself - Exception
> Is exempt from change.[3]

Emily Dickinson regarded death as the great unknown and never ceased to ponder its fascination and mystery. Death was the only one who remained unknown in his hometown. She remarks that death's parents were unknown and death grew up without playmates:

> Dust is the only secret
> Death, the only one
> You cannot find out all about
> In his "native" town
> Nobody knew his father -
> Never was a Boy -
> Hadn't any playmates -
> or Early History.[4]

Emily Dickinson thought of death and pondered over it constantly, she probed death daily and we might say she died all her life. Ultimately the obsession became morbid and she developed an excessive desire to know the details how a particular individual had died.

The earliest intimate experience of death in the life of Emily Dickinson came in April, 1844, when she was just thirteen. Sophia Holland, fifteen-year daughter of a neighbour was stricken fatally. Young Emily of thirteen watched the death of the girl whom she greatly admired. The untimely death of Sophia left Emily in a 'Fixed melancholy'. Her letter to Abiah Root depicts how deeply she was shattered at the demise of Sophia:

> I have never lost but one friend near my age and with whom my thoughts and her own were the same. It was

> before you came to Amherst. My friend was Sophia Holland ... I visited her often in sickness and watched over her bed. But at length the doctor said she must die and allowed me to look at her a moment through the over door. I took off my shoes and stole softly to the sick room. There she lay mild and beautiful as in her health and her pale features lit up with an unearthly smile. I looked as long as friends, I let them lead me away. I shed no tear for my heart was too full to weep but after she was laid in her coffin and I felt I could not call her back again, I gave way to a fixed melancholy. I told no one the cause of my grief, though it was growing at my very heart strings ...[5].

Emily Dickinson was too immature to realize why she had insisted on staying in the sick room as long as friends would permit. This oddly sensitive child felt the physical incident of death and established new perspective for the living and the phenomena of death.

This was her first confrontation with what she called, in later years, a hideous, inequitable mistake. Later she saw the death of her father who was one of the shaking influences of her life and her mother who had remained invalid for many years prior to her death, matched and nursed by her. She suffered the death of dear and near friends and relatives. The most important incident which gave her a sense of the immediacy of death was the demise of young Ben Newton, who in 1848 was living with her family as her father's law-apprentice. He was a brilliant, free thinker. The impact of this promising youngman on the adolescent mind of Emile Dickinson was deep enough to hold the promise of a romantic affair of the heart, if Newton had survived. But Providence had ordained otherwise and Newton died in the prime of life, leaving Emily Dickinson stunned. The traumatic effect of Newton's death was unlike the reaction of an inherent thirteen year old girl to her friend. This time Emily Dickinson's reaction was profounder, more grimly thoughtful, making her more philosophically aware of "Death" as a perplexing and puzzling phenomenon of life.

Another important factor which inspired Emily Dickinson to choose Death as an important subject for her poetry was the location of her home. The house, where the family of Emily Dickinson had shifted, faced the graveyard. Emily Dickinson, sitting near her window-pane, in her solitary upstairs room, daily watched innumeral funeral processions, going to the graveyard. She gazed and gazed at such funeral processions which left an everlasting impression on the mind of Emily Dickinson.

Thus since her early adolescent age, when Emily Dickinson watched her friend, Sophia Holland slowly dying, death remained throughout her life an over-mastering obsession. The five hundred and odd poems which deal with death, occupy a central place in the corpus of her poetry. No other event of life, no other object of contemplation pre-occupied her creative mind so much as the termination of man's earthly existence. No doubt, death has been a fascinating subject for other poets also: but Emily Dickinson stands out among them owing to her bold and thoroughly personal ideas about it. She has looked at it from various angles and described it in a poetic idiom of her own. "She died all her life, "says a critic emphasizing her persistent probings into its nature. Sometimes she would be enthralled by the peace and serenity that she saw on the face of the dead. Sometimes she would be shockingly intrigued and would almost echo the message of the Bibles:

O Death here is thy sting,
O Grave here is thy victory.

Sometimes Emily Dickinson seemed to ridicule the victory of the grave and ignored the sting of death. As she grew up her broodings over death became deeper and more chilling . In one of her letters she remarks that she feels that maturing only enhances mystery and never decreases it. Mystery deepens as maturity advances.

A large number of poems of Emily Dickinson on death are woven with one persistent thought. Such poems depict the physical demise of the body. They reveal that death breaks away the ties of communication with those who are on earth and creates mystery, intensity and uncertainty in the mind of all mortals whether that communication can ever be restored. In 1864, Emily Dickinson wrote :

Those who have been in the grave the longest-
Those who begin Today-
Equally perish from our Practice-
Death is the further way-
Foot of the Bold did least attempt it-
It - is the White Exploit-
Once to achieve annuls the power
Once to communicate[6]

In this poem, Emily Dickinson points out the fact that time does not matter. Time, which is the most important factor for those who are on earth, is valueless for those who reach the region of death. She says that those who die today or those who died long ago equally perish. Death makes no distinction for the "Bold" or the meek. It is the "White Exploit". It is the final deed done by man on earth, never to be repeated for it destroys man's capacity to act further. But she believes that:

I know that he exists
Some wherein silence.
He has bid her rare life
From our gross eye ....[7]

On the one hand, she acknowledges the physical demise on earth, on the other, she is confident of the fact that the dead person's soul still resides somewhere in silent distant land, invisible to the eyes of the mortals on the earth. The migration from the known world of ours to the unknown world after death is just a matter of trice and from the agony of the world, the dead man is transported to a blissful state which is the reward that he wins for the travail of death. But while the dead enjoys a state of blessedness, the physical decomposition, the *rigor - mortis* envelops the kith and kin of the dead in sorrow. One of Emily Dickinson's poems, written on the theme of death, runs as follows:

As by the dead we love to sit,
Because so wonderous dear,
As far the lost we grapple,

Though all the rest are here -
In broken mathematics
We estimate our prize
Vast, in its fading ratio,
To our curious eye;[8]

The above poem also deals with the subject of Death, leading ultimately to Immortality. All mortal beings tend to be close to the person, who is about to leave this physical world; and when he breathes his last, a great void is created through his absence. The departed soul is released from the closet of this mortal world and merges with much vaster realm of eternity. Hence it becomes beyond the capacity of his kinsmen to judge and estimate his relation to the heavenly abode.

While composing poems, throughout, Emily's mind was haunted by the sweet and painful memories of her dear and near ones, who departed to the heaven in the prime of their age. Her poems on death, evolved from the over powering emotion; rising in her heart and hence have a direct relation with the life which she lived. She writes :

A book, I have a friend gave
Whose pencil, here and there
Had notched the place and pleased her
At rest his fingers are.
Now when I read, I read not
For interrupting tears
Obliterate the etchings
Too costly for repairs.[9]

They recall everything when he was alive, the deeds done by him, the thing presented by him. In his life time, this dead friend gave a book marked here and there is pencil. But today when they pick up the book to read, they find themselves in the state of extreme sorrow and grief for the dead. The falling of their tears might remove the etchings which are so costly now and which they want to preserve as their valuable treasure.

Emily Dickinson is greatly intrigued and perplexed by the abrupt ending of life which in a trice makes a tremendous change:

To-day or this noon
She dwelt so close
I almost touched her;
To night she lies
Past neighbourhood -
And bough and steeple
Now past surmise.[10]

The dead grows totally oblivious of the surroundings in which he had lived and here lies the rut: In other poems she says-

The world feels dusty
When we stop to die
We want the dew then
Honour taste dry.
Mine be the Ministry
Why thy thirst comes
Dews of thyself to fetch
And holy balms.[11]

She pleads in this poem for some share in the moment of death of the others. To a dying person, every glamour of the earth appears to be dull, and colourless. He hardly cares for the public honour. His last and the only wish centres round the love of his friends for which he still preserves the thirst. His quench for such love, can be satisfied with the help of the tears of love which serve as holy balm. Emily Dickinson is eager to quench the thirst of the dead by giving her tribute of tears and in this respect she would be performing the ministry of love which she considers much more meaningful than the religious ministry. Therefore for Emily Dickinson-

If anybody's friend be dead
It is the sharpest of the theme -
The thinking how they walked alive
At such and such a time,
How pleased they were at what you send,
You try to touch the smile,
And dip your fingers in the frost,
When was it, can you tell.[12]

Death is the natural end of life. It dissolves the man in dust. Hence nothing belonging to the dead, whether it is walk, or smile can be preserved. On the other hand, all the past interviews, vows and promises made by the deceased fill the heart with sorrow and a heavy sense of loss.

Thus the lines quoted above prove that Emily Dickinson wrote poems not only in the capacity of an observer but her soul also seemed to be totally tormented and tortured by the spectacle of the death to such a degree that sometimes she vicariously experienced death.

In some poems, Emily Dickinson shows that death is not a subject of fear or fright. It is the natural end of human life. Instead of inflicting any injury, it liberates the man from agony, trials and tribulations, sorrow and sufferings that the body is an heir to. That is why she writes:

> To die takes just a little while-
> They say it doesn't hurt;
> It's only fainter by degrees,
> And then - its out of sight.
> The absent, mystic, creature
> That but for love of us
> Had gone to sleep that soundest time
> Without the weariness.[13]

This poem dwells upon the serene aspect of the process of dying. Unlike some other poems in which Emily Dickinson refers to the torment of death or the agony of witnessing a dear-one passing away, this poem is characterized by a quiet contemplation of death as it extinguishes life slowly and painlessly. Death here acts as an invisible foster mother or nurse that lulls the dying person into eternal slumber with the mundane scenes growing fainter and then vanishing. The abrupt end of life, i.e. death, is an ordinary, simple painless thing. Another poem of Emily Dickinson bearing the same vein of thought runs as follows:

> The dying need but little - dear
> A glass of water's all

A flower's unobtrusive face
To punctuate the wall.
A fan, perhaps a friend's regret
And certainly that one
No color in the rainbow
Perceives when you are gone.[14]

Dying is a natural and easy act. It does not go through any torturous process. The dying man spies a flower in the vase against the wall and then soon it grows invisible to him. He calls for a glass of water, takes a draught or two, and with it, breathes his last. Neither the fan which is being moved to cool his forehead, nor the regret of the friends, nor the colours of rainbow are visible to him. There is the blending of nostalgic feeling for the dead and the sad irony that we forget the one whom we had loved.

For Emily Dickinson, Death is not a bugbear of which man should be afraid. It is the natural end of life, and instead of inflicting pain on man, it protects him from the miseries and sufferings. A man buried in the tomb is no doubt safer than the man who is living and he has to face all sorts of troubles and hardships at the hands of his fellowmen and nature.

The clouds their Backs together laid.
The north began to push
The forests galloped till they fell
The lightning skipped like mice:
How good to be safe in tombs
Where nature's temper cannot reach
Nor Vengeance even comes ![15]

Thus the poet seems to have full confidence in the fact that Death is inevitable and it is the safest place for an individual, keeping him away from the reach of natural calamities or human exploitation. One can enjoy peaceful repose and sleep in one's tomb, far away from the chaos and confusion of this mortal world. Similarly in "The Last Night That She Lived" also death is imagined as a graceful departure into the sublime waters of immortality. Pain recedes as the dead woman obtains eternal peace.

Moreover, death is a source of wishfulfilment. Things which are unattainable in the real life, can be obtained in the life hereafter. Therefore she writes :

> If I may have it when it is dead
> I will contented be ;
> If just as soon as breath is out
> It shall belong to me.
> Until they lock it in the grave
> 'Tis bliss I cannot weigh
> For through they lock thee in the grave
> Myself can hold the key.[16]

The thought of the death of some dear and near one does not vex Emily because she believes that though the dead person will be buried in the grave, yet she can carry the key to reach the grave, i.e. through the key of her introspective vision and love, she will be able to communicate with the dead, resting in the grave. The poem offers a fruitful comparison with Browning's poem on the same theme, "Prospice". In this poem, Browning has presented a lover as a brave man, who would like to face the fury, pain and tortures caused by death boldly. He faced the struggle of life like the heroes of ancient days:

> I was ever a fighter, so - one fight more,
> The best and the last.
> I would hate that death bandaged my eye, and forbore,
> And bade me creep past
> No; let me tasts the whole of it, fare like my peers
> The heroes of old.

Throughout her life, Emily Dickinson was so much engrossed with the concept of death that she considered grave as her cottage. She writes -

> The grave my little cottage is
> Where keeping house for these,
> I make my parlor orderly
> And lay the marble tea
> For two divided, briefly
> A cycle it may be,
> Till everlasting life unites
> In strong society.[17]

This poem also has a touch of a confident hope of meeting of the two souls after the cycle of the birth and death, such as expressed by Browning in his poem, "Evelyn Hope." Thus death has been shorn of the feeling of terror which is usually associated with it. When the brief cycle of birth and death will be over, the two lovers will be united together in the celestial company. The idea is typically Indian in origin. It may be observed here that through Thoreau and Emerson, the ancient Indian philosophy became popular in America and the two philosophical ideas, current in America then, namely transcendentalism and Unitarianism, were derived from the ancient Hindu thought.

Death, as a big leveler and a democrate which occurs in some poems of the sixteenth and seventeenth centuries, has been described by Emily Dickinson in the peculiarly modern idioms. Death is in fact the great democrate who levels down all differences and obliterates all distinctions of rank and age. As before law, all are equal before Death.

Not any higher stands the rave
For heroes than for man
Not any nearer for the child
Than number three score and ten.[18]

Death makes no distinction between the high and the low, poor or the rich, instead it levels down all distinction of rank and age. Death is here synonymous to an inexorable cosmic law.

The latest leisure equal lulls
The beggar and his queen;
Propitiate his democrate
A Summer's afternoon.[19]

Death according to Emily Dickinson is a source of providing respite from toil and tears and the renewal of a new life for the soul.

It not only provides leisure and a well-deserved rest after the strenuous life on earth, and is thus a period of relaxation from toil, but it also is an opening for new life. Believing in soul's immortality. Emily Dickinson believes that death is not the end in life. It is simply a suspension of activity for a short while, after which the soul, having renewed its energy through rest, starts its new life. Death, therefore, symbolizes the beginning of a new life.

A death blow is life wow to some
Who, till they died, did not alive become
Who, had they lived, had died, but when
They died, vitality begun.

Death is a spiritual regenerator, a process of the revitalization of the soul. Shelley, in "Adonais", also expresses the idea of a new and more glorious life after death. He has rightly remarked that 'it is death that dies'. Donne has also expressed the same idea when he wrote, 'Death, thou shalt die'. This idea can further be found in Longfellow's poem "A Psalm of Life".

Dust thou art, to dust returnest
But that was not spoken of the soul.

The soul is never injured or hurt. It remains immortal. Therefore, why should man be vexed with the question of death? Death in fact symbolizes the beginning of new life -

A death blow is a life blow to some
Who till they died, did not alive become.[20]

Death, therefore, is nothing but a comfortable long sleep, replenishing the energies of the exhausted soul, in the long journey of life. In one of her poems she reflects -

A long, long sleep, a famous sleep
That makes no show of dawn
By stretch of limbs or stir of lid
An independent one.[21]

The same idea occurs in one of the poems of W.B. Yeats. He wrote:

A great man in his pride
Confronting murderous men
Casts decision upon
Supersession of breath;
He knows death to the bone -
Man has created death.[22]

Emily Dickinson holds the view that we should shun all our fears and misconception regarding the severity and sternity of God, who punishes man after death. She says -

Afraid ? of whom as I afraid ?
Not death, for who is he ?
The porter of my father's lodge
As much abasheth me.[23]

This poem bears strong resemblance with Browning's poem "Prospice" which begins thus -

Fear death ? To feel the fog in the throat ? ...

Therefore it would be wrong on our part to fear death, instead we should welcome it. She writes -

It feels a shame to be alive
When men so brave are dead.[24]

Persons who are really, great and virtuous, anticipate life after death and anxiously wait for their death boldly:

So proud she was to die
It made us all ashamed
So satisfied to go
Where none of us should be
Immediately - that Auguish stooped
Almost to Jealousy-[25]

Such virtuous people realize the futility and mortality of the physical world, and live in the world without any attachment or temptations. They know the fact that death is not the end of life. It is merely suspension of activities for a time, which renews the exhausted energies of the soul - and hence it starts new life. There are clear echoes of the ideas expressed in the Bhagwat Gita -

वासासि जीर्णानि यथा विहाय,
नवानि गृह्णाति नरोऽपराणि।
तथा शरीराणि विहाय जीर्णा,
न्यन्यानि संयाति नवानि देही।।
– "गीता"

Therefore we should not be afraid of death but should be proud to die and welcome death whole - heartedly. In the poem, cited above, Emily Dickinson recalls the incident of the death of her friend, Sophia; who showed no sign of sorrow, anguish, grief or agony when death approached her at an early age. Such heroic attitude to death made her friends feel envious because of her unruffled calm at the time of her death. A moment ago, the same friends were stricken with sorrow for her physical demise. Therefore Emily Dickinson is also ready to depart from this world, unmindful of the trials and tribulations that one has to undergo at the time of death. She writes -

> Tie the strings to my life, My Lord
> Then, I am ready to go;
> Goodbye to the Life I used to live
> And the world I used to know -
> And kiss the Hills, for me, just once -
> Then - I am ready to go;[26]

Emily Dickinson willingly and joyfully bids farewell to the world she lived and makes every preparation for her journey to the immortal world. It is a welcome relief from the mortal ills. It is the blessed means to eternal happiness. Thus death frees man from the pangs of sufferings and sorrow on one hand, while on the other hand creates a heavy sense of loss in the mind and heart of the poetess. One terror related to death obsessed her mind i.e. the event of death left her irrecoverable out of touch with those she had loved. In 1864, such idea issued from her -

> Death leaves us homesick, who behind
> Except that it is gone
> Are ignorant of its concern
> As if it were not born[27]

In the same year, Emily wrote the poem - A Coffin-is a small Domain," dealing with Death. Here she says that Death ultimately leads to Coffin, which apparently "Small" in Domain" yet able to contain "a citizen of Paradise", "In its diminished Plane." Though it has a "restricted Breadth" yet its scope is vaster than the area lit by the rays of the sun. The people outside grave are totally ignorant of the surroundings and the wail and woes that the deceased has to face in his grave. Sometimes Emily seems to lose courage and gets nervous and puzzled at the thought of Death. In "A Clock Stopped" she describes the moment of death when the heart ceases to beat and no physician's skill can restore life. The second stanza of this poem goes back to the moment before death when the dying person, hunched with pain, realizes an awful moment at hand.

> An awe came on the Trunk lit
> The Figures hunched, with pains -
> Then quirered out of Decimals-
> Into Degreeless Noon-[28]

Any Death for Emily Dickinson was experience which she too shared and the death of friends was one in which she emotionally participated. Thus it is clear that she witnessed death from two directions, through the eyes of an observer and through the sensations of a dying man. In fact, there are some lyrics on death in which Emily graphically presents the sensations and physical experiences, the man endures at the time of his death. In some lyrics, Emily has vividly presented the final acts of a dying person. She was so much engrossed with the conception of death that at times, while sitting at the window-pane of her topmost solitary room of her home, she imagined her own death. How beautifully she puts the process through which she would undergo before reaching the unknown region of death:

> I heard a fly buzz - when I died
> The stillness in the Room
> Was like the stillness in the Air-
> Between the Heaves of storm-[29]

The poem is remarkable for the poet's imaginative power and her keen and sensitive observation of what happens to the dying man. Here Emily Dickinson attains a degree of 'Negative-Capability', which takes her quite near to the sensations and physical experience of the dying man. The picture and the images used are so apt and clear that they present the exact scenes before us. In the present poem, the tension is established by the contrast between the inertness of the dead person with the movement of the living and the external growth of Nature. The traditional Christian belief that death leads to eternal happiness seems to be contradicted by the appearance of an insignificant fly coming at the grand moment. In other words, the poem, quoted above satirizes the traditional view of death as a peaceful release from life's pressures and glorious entry into the immortality. Similarly the following poem is a distinct picture of disturbing portrayal of death:

I felt a funeral in my Brain
And Mourners to and fro
Kept treading - treading till it seemed
The sense was breaking through[30]

Similarly the above poem 'I felt a funeral in my Brain' is an even more disturbing portrayal of death. There is no hope of immortality in this poem also. It depicts a despairing plunge into an eternal abyss.

Since Emily Dickinson participated in the death of every near and dear one mentally, emotionally and psychologically, a very clear and vivid picture of such scenes is retained in her mind and she writes :

There's been a death in the opposite house
As lately as to-day,
I know it by the numb look
Such house have-aways-
The neighbours rustle in and out -
The doctor - drives away -
A window opens like a pod, -
Abrupt - mechanically.[31]

Thus Emily Dickinson witnessed death from two directions : through the eyes of an observer and through the sensations of a dying man. Poems such as "How many times these low fee staggered and "I have seen a Dying Eye" are composed from the point of view of one who stands alone in a room, gazing at the dead body e.g.

How many times these low feet staggered-

Only the soldered mouth can tell-
Try - can you stir the awful rivet-
Try - can you lift the hasps of steel!

The above poem explores the terrible physical transformation caused by death. Only images of iron and stone recall this once vital soul. Yet in the final stanza, death brings a release from pain and guilt, and frees one from the monotonous toil of sewing and dusting.

Similarly, in the poem quoted below, Emily Dickinson stands as a detached observer, viewing death and its effects.

Thus "I've seen a Dying Eye captures the feverish intensity of a dying person's for a "something" which is found without ever being disclosed to the intent onlooker. Thus death continues to baffle all human efforts to comprehend its meaning.

I've seen a dying eye
Run round and round a room-
In search of something - as it seemed
The cloudier became-
And then - obscure with Fog-
And then - he soldered down
Without disclosing what it be
'Twere blessed to have seen[32]

There are other poems of Emily Dickinson which have a strong elegiac note, since they are expressions of personal sorrow or the loss of some near and dear one. According to Thomas H. Johnson-

"The elegies that Emile wrote as a tribute to the memory of persons she had loved range in quality from that least to the finest of her creations — The greater number of the commemorative poems were sent to friends on the occasion of a bereavement ..."[33]

I meant to find her, when I come
Death had the same design;
But the success was his, it seems,
And the discomfit mine.[34]

This poem is an impassioned expression of sorrow, occasioned by the death of her friend. She had gone there to see her friend alive but death had pre-empted her and she was not vouchsafed to bid goodbye to her departing friend. This sorrow will continue to rankle in her mind and to still the voice of inner anguish she will have to forego rest throughout her life. Arnold's poem, "Requiescat", bears close resemblances with the above poem. Arnold in the above poem celebrates the death of a girl named Margaret, *who was tired of the wearisome burden of life.*

Emily Dickinson was sorrow stricken, when her mother's favourite sister, Lavinia Norcross, died in Boston in April, 1860. She sent an eight-line verse to the motherless teen-age cousins, Louse and Fraces-

Mama never forgets her birds
Thou' in another tree,
She looks down just as often
And just as tenderly
As when her little mortal next
With causing care she wore
If either of her "Sparrows fall,"
She "notices" above.[35]

Similarly, she wrote a poem in memory of Charlotte Bronte, where Bronte is described as a bird-

Some Days retired from the rest
In soft distinction lie
Or was delighted to die.[36]

In this small poem, Emily Dickinson contrasts two distinct days; one that brought her friend to her and other when her friend died. In this way the day of death can be singled out in a sharp contrast against other days because it is associated with the death of a friend. Her father's death on 16th June, 1874, fixed that date in her memory and was the occasion for several elegies. In a letter to Mrs. Holland, she wrote the following unforgettable sentence:

"Mother is asleep in the Library - Vinnie-in the Dining Room-Farther - in the Maked Bed in the Most-House."[37] She continues:

How soft his prison is -
How sweet those sullen Bais.
No Despot - but the kind of Dawn.
Invented that Repose;[38]

In March 1876, she wrote to Colonel Higginson with greater emotional effect:

When I think of my father's lovely life a lovelier Death, there is this redress-

Take all away -
The only thing worth larceny
Is left the Immortality.[39]

In mid June 1877, Emily Dickinson wrote to Colonel Higginson in a pensive mood and dedicated her tribute to her father in the following words :

Lay this laurel on the one
Too intrinsic for renown
Laurel - veil your deathless fate
Him you Chasten - that is He;[40]

Again in 1882, Emily Dickinson got an occasion to write one poem at the news of the death of her mother and Charles Wadsworth :

Obtaining but our own extent
In whatsoever Realm-
Twas Christ own personal Expanse
That bore him from the Tomb-[41]

There were still two more distressing bereavements, which she had to face. When Judge Lord died in 1884, she composed three elegies in his memory : "Go thy great way," "Through the great Winter Sleep" and "Quite empty, quite at rest." The last poem is as follows :

Quite empty, quite at rest
The Robin locks her Nest, and tries her wings
She does not know a Route
But puts her craft absent.[42]

The last poem from her pen came in 1886. Colonel Higginson wrote a sonnet in memory of Helen Jackson and sent to Emily. She went through the copy of the sonnet and added -

> The Immortality she gave
> We borrowed at her grave.
> For just one plaudit famishing
> The might of Human love-[43]

Apart from these personal elegies, Emily has also written some impersonal elegies on human mortality. She living a cloistered, fugitive life, sitting at her window pane, must have visualized cornfields and various activities going on in the fields e.g. sifting of grain from husk. Such scene at once struck her mind with the idea of death and the separation of the soul from the mortal body:

> Midsummer was it when they died-
> A full and perfect time-
> The summer closed upon itself
> In consummated bloom-
> The corn her furthest kernel field
> Before the coming flail-
> When there - learned into perfectness-
> Through haze of burial-[44]

Here she compares the ripe corn fields with innumerable graves, she viewed from her window-pane. Human beings, when they attain perfection of maturity, die, and the soul leaves their body, which is now worthless; So is the case with the ripe grain.

We can take another example of the impersonal elegy when Emily Dickinson laments the death of those who die unadmired, unsung and unhonoured:

> How many flowers fail in wood-
> Or perish from the hill
> Without the privilege to know
> That they are beautiful -
> How many cast a nameless Pad
> Upon the nearest breeze -
> Unconscious of the scarlet freight -
> It bears to other eyes-[45]

The above poem of Emily Dickinson bears close affinity with Gray's "Elegy written in a Country Church yard", where he too mourns the tragic fate of the villagers who fail to avail themselves of the opportunities to make a mark and thus die without displaying their talents, traits and merits-

Full many a gem of purest ray serene
The dark, unfathomed caves of ocean bear
Full many a Flower is born to blush unseen
And waste its sweetness on the desert air.

Quite a number of poems follow different manner and vein, with death figuring as a person, nebulous creature at first, develops the status of true character of fiction. In 1859 she wrote - "One dignity for all" in which she depicts Death as a potentate, property attended and escorted by persons belonging to different rank.

Triumph - may be of several kinds-
There's Triumph in the Room
When that old Imperator - Death
By Faith - he over come-[46]

The above poem, written in 1862, is the last poem in which Emily Dickinson imagines death as a swollen tyrant. The figure of death as an old Imperator may be compared with Browning's "Arch Fear" in Prospice.

In 1860, Emily wrote another poem, in which she has given beautiful description of Death, where it is personified, having its own "Native town" whose "Father" "playmates" or any paces of "Early History" is beyond the understanding of the mortals on the earth. The first two stanzas of the poem run as follow:

Dust is the only secret-
Death, the only one
You cannot find out all about
In his "native town,"
Nobody know his "Father"-
Never was a Boy-
Hadn't any playmates,
or "Early History."[47]

Thus Death, which has been Portrayed having a full-fledged personality and existence remains a secret and mystery to those who have not reached the region of Death.

In 1864, Emily came forth with another poems on the theme of death, where Death is described as 'the White Exploit'-

> Foot of the Bold did least attempt at
> It - is the White Exploit-

One of the best poems on the theme of Death in which Death came into full stature as a person, is "Because I could not stop for Death" or "Chariot". It is a superlative achievement wherein death becomes one of the greatest characters of literature. The poem beautifully handles the effects of death's unexpected visit upon the victim. According to Allen Tate-

> The terror of death is objectified through the figure of the genteel driver, who is made ironically to serve the end of Immortality. This is the heart of the poem. She has presented a typical Christian theme in its final irresolution without making any final statements about it .... the idea of Immortality is confronted with the fact of physical disintegration. We are not told what to think. We are told to look at the situation.[48]

In this particular poem, Emily visualized Death as a person she knew and trusted. This person might be any person from Amherst, or any tutor, minister of lawyer, whom she knew and with whom she exchanged valentines and who at one trial or another had acted as her lover, well-wisher-

> Because I could not stop for Death-
> He kindly stopped for me-
> The Carriage held, but just ourselves
> And Immortality.[49]

The carriage holding Death and Emily Dickinson was on its way. It was a last Ride Together, so they drove in a leisurely manner, feeling completely at ease. The poetess was so busy that she could not possibly have taken time to wait for him; Death, her lover, out of politeness stopped for her to take her. She, therefore, puts her work aside to spare her moments in the company of her kind visitor-

We slowly drove. He knew no haste
And I had put away
My labour and my leisure too
For his civility-[50]

Then in the third stanza, she watches the routine of life she passes from, children playing games during a school recess. Then the motion quickens and quickly her eyes catch the sight of field of grains and the setting sun:

We passed the School, where children strove
At Recess - in the Ring -
We passed the Fields of Gazing Grain -
We passed the setting Sun-[51]

This stanza shows Emily Dickinson's power to fuse into a single order of perception, a heterogeneous series; the children, the grain and the setting Sun.

The last two stanzas of the poem lead to the final identification of her "House" which is like a swelling of the ground, hardly visible. All the motions and actions by now cease to exist. She recalls the last objects before her eyes during the journey; the heads of the horses that bore her, were towards eternity :

We paused before a House that seemed
A Swelling of the Ground -
The Roof was scarcely visible -
The Cornice - in the Ground -
Since then - 'tis Centuries - and yet
Feels shorter than the Day
I first surmised the Horses Head
Were towards Eternity.[52]

Gradually as we come to the last two stanzas of the poem, we realize that Death, as a person had reached into the background after leading the poetess to the threshold of Immortality.

In this poem, every image is precise, not merely beautiful but also fused with the central idea. It is this poem where Emily Dickinson's views on Death and Immortality reach artistic perfection.

Apart from this well-known poem, there is another important poem of Emily Dickinson, "Death is the Supple Suitor," where she, describes death as a gentleman, visitor or lover. She wrote in 1878 :

Death is the Supple Suitor
That wins at last-
It is a stealthily Wooing
Conducted first ....
It bears away in triumph
To Troth unknown
And kindered as responsive
As celain.[53]

Thus for Emily Dickinson, Death assumes various roles. It comes like an accommodating civil, courteous pilot leading human soul kindly to the shore of Eternity, where there is undisturbed peace and everlasting happiness :

On this wondrous Sea
Sailing silently
Knowest thou the shore
Ho pilot, ho
Knowest thou the shore
Where no breakers roar-
Where the storm is o'er?[54]

Like Emily Dickinson, Ravindra Nath Tagore has also composed a number of poems on the subject of death, although his attitude to death differs from Dickinson's attitude. There are however some images that are common. Both the poets have described death as a journey to an unknown land. Tagore observes in Kanika :

On this tiny raft
I shall cross the river of life ....
When the twilight descends
I shall discard and heed it no more
Let it drift away.
Then what shadows, what light[55]

Similarly, both the poets, regard death as a visitor, lover, suitor; Death as a kind visitor appears in Tagore in more than one poems:

"Death thy servant is at my door/He has crossed the unknown sea and brought thy call to my home."

And again in song no. ninety of *Gitanjali* he sings-

On this day when death will knock
at thy door, what wilt thou offer to him?
Oh, I will set before my guest the
full vessel of my life - I will never
Let him go with empty hands ....[56]

The above discussion leads us to conclude that death is a major theme in Emily Dickinson's poetry. She is so much obsessed with the conception death that at times it becomes almost a morbid interest.

Emily Dickinson was a seeker after truth and in proving the mystery of death, she has defined the limits of human knowledge. She viewed her doom and the doom of all mankind without fear. Like Kabir, Emily Dickinson is also aware of the futility and mortality of this world. She is well-acquainted with the stark reality that the existence of a human being is subject to. Life, here is as temporary and short-lived as the bubbles of water and the fast-disappearing stars of early morning. Her approach to death is ontological as she presents it as eternal silence of stillness and even as darkness. Death is a final and faithful companion.

REFERENCES

1. Thomas H. Johnson (ed.), *The Complete Poems of Emily Dickinson*, (Delhi, Kalyani Publishers, 1960), Poem No. 759, p. 372.
2. *Ibid.*, Poem No. 698, p. 344.
3. *Op. cit.*, Poems No. 749, p. 367.
4. *Ibid.*, Poem No. 153, p. 72.
5. Thomas H. Johnson, *Emily Dickinson, Interpretative Biography* (U.S.A., Harvard University Press, 1967), p. 205.
6. Johnson, *The Complete Poems*, Poem No. 922, pp. 433-434.
7. *Ibid.*, Poem No. 338, p. 160.

8. *Ibid.*, Poem No. 88, pp. 44-45.
9. *Ibid.*, Poem No. 360, pp. 170-171.
10. *Ibid.*, Poem No. 1702, p. 693.
11. *Ibid.*, Poem No. 715, p. 351.
12. *Ibid.*, Poem No. 509, pp. 247-248.
13. *Ibid.*, Poem No. 255, pp. 116-117.
14. *Ibid.*, Poem No. 1026, pp. 471-72.
15. *Ibid.*, Poem No. 1172, p. 521.
16. *Ibid.*, Poem No. 577, pp. 281-82.
17. *Ibid.*, Poem No. 1743, pp. 706-707.
18. *Ibid.*, Poem No. 1256, p. 550.
19. *Idem.*
20. *Ibid.*, Poem No. 816, p. 397.
21. *Ibid.*, Poem No. 654, p. 326.
22. W.B. Yeats, *Collected Poems* (London: Macmillan, 1950), p. 264.
23. Martha Dickinson Bianchi and Alfred Leete Hampson (eds.) Poems by Emily Dickenson (Little Brown Company, 1952), p. 167.
24. *Ibid.*, p. 322.
25. Martha and Leete Hampson, pp. 207-208.
26. *Ibid.*, p. 205.
27. Johnson (ed.), Poem No. 935, p. 39.
28. *Ibid.*, Poem No. 287, pp. 132-133.
29. *Ibid.*, Poem No. 465, p. 223.
30. *Ibid.*, Poem No. 280, p. 128.
31. *Ibid.*, Poem No. 389, p. 185.
32. *Ibid.*, Poem No. 547, p. 266.
33. Thomas H. Johnson, *Emily Dickinson: An Interpretative Biography.* (U.S.A., Harvard University Press, 1967), pp. 244-245.
34. Johnson, *Complete Works*, Poem No. 718, p. 353.
35. *Ibid.*, Poem No. 164, p. 77.
36. *Ibid.*, Poem No. 1157, pp. 516-517.
37. Thomas H. Johnson, *Emily Dickinson: An Interpretative Biography.* (U.S.A., Harvard University Press, 1967), p. 227.
38. Johnson, *Complete Works*, Poem No. 1334, p. 578.
39. *Ibid.*, Poem No. 1365, p. 588.
40. *Ibid.*, Poem No. 1393, p. 597.

41. Johnson, *op. cit.*, Poem No. 1543, p. 663.
42. *Ibid.*, Poem No. 1606, p. 663.
43. Johnson, *op. cit.*, Poem No. 1648, pp. 674-675.
44. *Ibid.*, Poem No. 962, p. 450.
45. *Ibid.*, Poem No. 404, p. 192.
46. *Ibid.*, op. cit., Poem No. 455, p. 219.
47. *Ibid.*, Poem No. 153, p. 72.
48. Allen Tate: Death in Emily Dickinson, *The Emily Dickinson Journal*, 6, 2 (1997), p. 21.
49. *Ibid.*, Poem No. 712, p. 350.
50. *Idem.*
51. *Idem.*
52. *Idem.*
53. *Ibid.*, Poem No. 1445, p. 614.
54. *Ibid.*, Poem No. 4, pp. 6-7.
55. R.N. Tagore, *Gitanjali* (Song Offerings), (Delhi, Macmillan & Co. Ltd., 1949), Poem No. 86.
56. *Ibid.*, Song No. 90, p. 79.

IMMORTALITY

5

How firm Eternity must look
To crumbling men like me
The only Adamant Estate
In all Identity.[1]

Just as Death is the gateway to Immortality, in the same way, the death poems of Emily Dickinson end only to usher in a new phase in her poetical career. The dominant mood of this phaze is a searching inquiry into the belief in Immortality, its nature and the necessity of such a belief as a Corollary to death. In her thoughts on Immortality, we find the streaks of transcendentalism as shaped by the ancient Hindu faith in the transmigration of soul running through the Biblical love which forms the background of her religious culture. Emily Dickinson views and examines death through the spectrum of varying moods, situations and feelings. She looks at the problem of the soul-survival and the problem of eternity from different angles. The faith in Immortality, though rooted in her Puritan heritage, is more poetic theme than a theological statement and therefore the poems on this theme like the poems on Death reveal essentially her poetical character and personality.

The two intellectual and spiritual force that shaped Emily's thinking were the Puritan tradition into which she was born and the romantic and transcendental doctrines that were prevalent in the New England of her youth.

Emily Dickinson's belief in immortality is not free from doubts and she has freely expressed them in several of her poems. In one of her poems, she describes that she is finite and circumscribed by time, she could not comprehend the perfection and the glory of the eternal life to come.

> The House of supposition
> The glimmering Frontier that
> Skirts the Acres of Perhaps-
> To me - shows insecure-[2]

Heaven, thus is a house of supposition which exists in the mind of the poetess. It is not a place of concrete reality, but full of doubts and "acres of Perhaps", beyond the understanding of this "timid life of Evidence" - timid because it fails to project itself into the cosmos to explore the larger truths.

In another poem, Emily asks as to what place was better, this Heaven' of worldly existence or the heaven to come. Whatever drawbacks there may be in this world, at least it exists solidly and is free from the doubts of its existence. This is not so in the case of heaven. The choice, therefore, is very obvious but the poetess makes it further clear by employing the saying that a bird in hand is better than two in the bush:

> Which is best? Heaven -
> Or only Heaven to come
> . . . . . .
> With that old codicil of Doubt?
> I cannot help esteem
> The "Bird within the Hand"
> superior to the one
> The "Bush" may yield me
> Or may not
> Too late to choose again.[3]

In one of her poems, Emily Dickinson frankly expresses her view that heaven is only a pretention, and at the best, it is only a kind of Self-deception. For, the heaven is a symbol of depreciation, and life comes only once and does not return again:

> Of heaven above the firmest proof
> We fundamental know
> Except for it's marauding Hand
> It had been Heaven below.[4]

Emily Dickinson expressed her preference for the mortal life in one of her early poems:

Going to Heaven !
How dim it sounds ![5]

And then expressed her own view in unmistakable terms:

I'm glad I don't believe it
For it w'd stop my breath-
And I'd like to look a little more
At such a curious Earth![6]

There are two specific occasions when Emily Dickinson directly expressed her doubt in immortality. It was when she was confronted with tragedy in her personal life. After the death of her father who was one of the shaping forces in her life, her agonized comment on immortality reveal the fragile nature of her belief; "I am glad there is Immortality–" After the death of her mother, she wrote,

"We do not know where she is, though many tell us." But sometimes such confident notes issue from her mind:

The Life we have is very great
The Life that we shall see
Surpasses it, we know, because
It is Infinity.
But when all space has been beheld
And all Dominion shown
The smallest human Heart's extent
Reduces to none[7]

Human heart and mind are too small and limited to grasp the entire dimension of immortality. Emily Dickinson, therefore, employs the homely metaphor of two-storey building in which the first floor is mortality and the ground floor is immortality:

If my Bark sink
Tis to another sea -
Mortality's Ground Floor
Is Immortality.[8]

In the above poem, Emily Dickinson employs two equally valid metaphors, the sea and the house. The bark or the boat is the symbol for soul and its sinking signifies death. But the sinking leads to its existence on another sea - the sea of Immortality.

For Emily Dickinson, Death and Immortality were two distinct subjects. The poems written on the theme of Death exceed in number than the poems on Immortality. By 1862, her introspective insight and experience led her to the vision of "the Colossal Substance of Immortality."

> The Soul's superior instants
> Occur to Her - alone -
> When friend - and Earth's occasion
> Have infinite withdrawn -
> Eternity's disclosure
> To favourites - a few -
> Of the Colossal Substance
> Of Immortality.[9]

Here she expresses the idea that Immortality is vouchsafed only to a few, only to those who really deserve it. This thought is in resemblance with Calvin's Puritanistic theory. The glooming doctrines of Calvinism emphasizes that redemption is a matter of accident and cannot be claimed as a privilege even by those who practice extreme penance. Even then this doctrine enjoins upon all its followers to lead a strictly, ascetic life, keeping out all pleasure of the flesh. Emily Dickinson endeavoured to be acquainted with the idea of Immortality, so like Browning :

> I would hate that death bandaged my eyes and forbore,
> And bade me creep past.

She also hated death, bandaging her eyes and she looked upon the mystery of the unknowable with all faculties alert. In a letter to Higginson she wrote :

> You mention Immortality: That is the Flood Subject[10]
> Thomas H. Johnson writes -
> Her discoveries about the human heart were made as they always must be through travail and better self-appraisal.[11]

In 1860, Emily Dickinson expressed the view : "To learn the transport by the Pain : This is the sovereign Anguish;[12]

She is of the opinion that one has to suffer much for entering the region of Immortality and the suffering, such experience is of a high order.

Quite frequently, Emily Dickinson's resentment against the dogmas in which she had been trained pops up. She deadly revolted against the doctrine of infant domination, as did Oliver Wendell Holmes, who belonged to her father's generation. She could never reconcile to the God who punishes -

> Far from Love the Heavenly Father
> Leads the chosen child
> Oftener through Realm of Briar
> Than the Meadow mild.
> Oftener by the Claw of Dragon
> Than the Hand of Friend
> Guides the Little one predestined
> To the Native Land.[13]

The poetess shows her resentment to God, the Heavenly Father. Even the innocent children become the prey to His cruel-treatment. Instead of showing any mercy and putting the hand of kindness on them, He uses the Claw of Dragon to take them to His 'Native Land' i.e. the region of Immortality. At times she feels that the inanimate objects of nature are superior in their fate and plight to the human beings. The poem beginning "How Happy is the little stone," ironically concludes that inanimateness alone can be 'happy', because "it alone fulfills absolute decree."[14]

The orthodox community living in the Connecticut River Valley subscribed with a blind faith to the Doctrine of Original Sin which is the bed-rock of Christian theology. Their deep-rooted faith was further buttressed by the pulpit-sermons delibered off and on by the divines and clergymen in the churches but the conscience of Emily Dickinson nurtured and schooled under the Puritan faith, found it difficult to reconcile itself to this doctrine and Emily finally rejected it as a perverse ideas, implanted in the minds of young. She felt that the poor mortals suffer unlike the inanimate objects of nature, who lead a blissful existence unmolested by the divine love.

> Sin -a distinguished Prespice
> Others must resist -
> Boys that 'believe' are very lonesome -
> Other Boys are lost-[15]

Emily Dickinson's gradual withdrawl from church attendance and the world outside led her to explore more and more into the unknown region of Immortality. Her unique approach to the concept of Immortality is seen in the poem "This world is not conclusion" which she wrote in 1862. This poem expresses Emily Dickinson's positive faith in Immortality and God though generations have raked their brains and martyrs suffered tortures -

> This world is not conclusion
> A species stand beyond -
> Invisible as music -
> But positive as sound-[16]

Emily Dickinson says that the riddle of God and Immortality is still unsolved although philosophers and scholars have deeply contemplated over the subject and bold spirits have suffered in their endeavour to know the riddle. All their efforts are fruitless as the mystery still exists :

> Faith slips - and laughs, and rallies -
> Blushes, if any sea -
> Plucks at a twig or Evidence
> And ashs a vane, the way -
> Nacratice cannot still the Tooth
> That nibbles at the soul-[17]

In the above poem, Emily Dickinson throws light on the fact that doubt and mystery still exist regarding the validity of religious practice. "She felt a liberty in speaking to God about such double-dealing that she would never have presumed to take any human friend. For instance, what did God mean by creating man in his own image, infinite in reason, only to return him to dust:"[18]

A shade upon the mind there passes
As when on Noon
A cloud the mighty sun encloses
Remembering
That some there be too numb to notice
Oh God
Why give if Thou must take away
The Lord ?[19]

In an another poem she writes :

"Heavenly Father" - take to thee
The Supreme inquity .....
We apologize to thee
For thine own Duplicity-[20]

She jeers with mock politeness at the dual policy adopted by God. In her view, God does not deserve honour and still we defend His duplicity. Knowing His Duplicity, we justify His ways to man. She presents the image of God as all-seeing when she writes :

If God could make a visit -
Or ever took a Nap -
Perennial beholds us -
Myself would run away
From Him - Holy Ghost - and All-
But there's the "Judgement Day;"[21]

She says in the above poem that the all - seeing God always keeps a watch on us. One might have no faith in God or religion but one cannot escape it. When God is away from his abode or makes a visit or takes a Nap, and we try to run away from His custody, but we are sure to face the Day of Judgement. In one of her poems, she shows indifference on the part of God towards the human being -

Of course - I prayed
And did God care ?
He cared as much as on the Air
A Bird - had stamped her foot -
And cried "Give Me"[22]

Thomas H. Johnson, in 'An Interpretative Biography' of Emily Dickinson relates that one of the friends of Emily Dickinson, Maria Whitney, delayed in replying to her letter; which annoyed her. She compared her friend with God. We pray to Him and He answers "No". She had sometimes lacked faith in God and could not appreciate the planning and design of God, who being the 'Father' i.e. creator and survivor, Himself created so much of differences and distinction among various creatures. Inspired by such ideas she sometimes gets aggressive and writes-

Papa above;
Regard a Mouse
O'erpowered by the Cat;
Reserve within thy kingdom
A "Mansion" for the Rat;[23]

In the above poem, Emily Dickinson raises her voice in favour of those who are weak, down-trodden and deprived of the facilities available to others in abundance. Taking an ordinary example of cat and rat, she speaks in favour of the latter. Why has God not made any provision for the safely of the poor rat and has reserved all the powers of cat ?

There is some perversity in God's creation in the sense that there is none to protect the helpless and she calls upon God to protect all creatures, young and small and thus justify Himself being called 'Father' above - This poem offers a contrast to Browning's 'Pippa Passes' where he says:

God is in His heaven
All's right with the world.

Emily's attitude to God is typically modernist because of its non-conformistic and critical approach.

Sometimes Emily seems to taunt God for wooing the soul vicariously; God plays various roles, sometimes as stern dictator, sometimes a naughty boy, indulging in various mischief. The concluding lines of the poem "Over the fence Straw berries grew" support the idea, stated above :

But - if I stained my Apron-
H'd - climb - if He could.[24]

The poems discussed above depict Emily Dickinson's non-conformistic tendency. She was not a blind follower of some religion or God but held her individual attitude towards God, Eternity and Immortality.

Emily Dickinson's finest philosophic poem dealing with the relation between Eternity and Immortality is "Behind - Me dips Eternity." The poem focuses on the moment of death, when the soul hovers between chaos and eternity. Unlike her other poems this poem has a carefully-woven structure and consistent philosophy-

> Behind Me - dips Eternity -
> Before Me - Immortality -
> Myself - The Term between
> Death but the Drift of Eastern Gray,
> Dissolving into Dawn away,
> Before the West begin-[25]

This beautiful poem is her poetic testament of Immortality and reminds us of Wordsworth's "ode on Intimations of Immortality" where he says -

> "By trailing clouds of glory do we come
> From God, who is our home
> Heaven lies about us in our infancy."

The second stanza runs as follows:

> Tis Kingdoms-afterward-they say -
> In perfect - pauseless Monarchy -
> Whose Prince - is Son of None -
> Himself - His Dateless Dynasty -
> Himself - Himself diversify -
> In Duplicate divine-[26]

The Kingdom of Immortality is perfect, painless having no ancestor or successor; Dynasty is dateless. He is doubly divine, in the sense that He is both the creator and the created. The last stanza of this poem states that Immortality is a miracle, inexplanable by reason or science. Hence the riddle regarding Immortality lies unsolved.

"Love, faith, death, Immortality - the four diversions are the forces by which the willing creature is bound to the willing God

... Love goes infinitely beyond the grave, and we become better images of those we loved because we try to imitate them. Thus we are made willing to die.

Unable are the loved to die
For love is Immortality
Nay, it is Deity -"[27]

The poems of Emily Dickinson on the theme of Immortality present continuous repercussion in the mind of Emily. Sometimes she fails to accept the Omnipotence and her mind ceases to reconcile with the duplicate policies of the Almighty. Sometimes, she gains positive faith in God and Immortality.

By the year 1881, as her end drew nearer, Emily's meditation took a deeper religious hue. On the eve of Christ's Birth day, She wrote to Colonel Higginson :

The Saviour must have been
A docile Gentleman -
To come so far so cold a Day
For little Fellowmen-[28]

Emily Dickinson's firm faith in God and Immortality did not stem from religious teaching alone, but also from her own experience and musing on the mystery of life :

The grave my little cottage is,
Where keeping house for thee
I make my parlor orderly
And lay the marble tea.[29]

Emily Dickinson is so confident about the concept of Immortality that she anticipates her life after death. While residing in her grave, in the region of Immortality, she imagines herself to be quite at ease, totally comfortable, and relaxed and reserves seat for other friends also in this unique but "Orderly" set 'parlor'.

In the following poem, again we find Emily Dickinson in a state of extreme ecstasy as she anticipates the celestial joys. She writes :

Me - Come ! My dazzled face
In such a shining place !

Me-Hear My foreign ear
The sounds of welcome-near ![30]

Her debut in heaven is anticipated with great thrill, excitement and joy. Positive faith in God can be acquired through the sufferings and calamities that overtake human beings:

Immortal is an ample word
When what we need is by,
But when it leaves us for a time,
'Tis a necessity.[31]

Here she expresses a common phenomenon that we think of God only when we suffer or are stricken by misfortune. God and Immortality become a necessity for human beings, not because religious books teach us but because they help man come outside from the grip of misfortune and sufferings. She wrote in 1864 -

The only news I know
Is bulletins all day
From Immortality
The only shows I see
Tommorrow and To-day
Perchase Eternity
The only one I meet
Is God -[32]

Emily Dickinson in the above poem expresses her firm faith in Immortality, Eternity and God. She has full understanding of these three and is ignorant of other things. If she comes to know about fourth thing, then she would definitely communicate it with the world.

Immortality and God are invisible to us unless some calamity or danger befalls :

The soul's distinct connection
with immortality
Is best disclosed by danger,
Or quick calamity -
As lightning on a landscape

Exhibits sheets of place
Not yet suspected but for flash
And bolt and suddenness.[33]

Just as lightning brings to light the thing hidden from our view, in the same way, man becomes aware of his distinct connection with God and Immortality, only when he is stricken by misfortune. In another poem she says -

Omnipotence had not a tongue ;
His lisp is Lightning-and the Sun -
His conversion - with the sea -
"How shall you know ? "Consult your eye![34]

In the above poem, she points out the fact that the existence of God can be known not through religious terms and philosophical theories but by the intuition of a man. God has no tongue. He cannot speak. But our eyes can judge how and what all has been created in the world.

In the poem, beginning with "Suspense is hostiler than Death", Emily Dickinson clearly expresses the view that death ultimately leads to Immortality. She writes -

Suspense is hostiler than Death,
Suspense does not conclude,
But perishes to live anew,
But just a new to die,
Annihilation plated fresh
With Immortality.[35]

Death is superior to suspense. Death leads one to its destination, i.e. Immortality, while suspense which never perishes, makes man perpetually perplexed and disturbed. Death, on the other hand, is a means to a sublime end, i.e. Immortality.

Therefore, Death of any person should not be mourned. She writes -

If tolling bell I ask the cause,
"A soul has gone to God,"
I'm answered in a lonesome tone:
Is heaven then so sad ?
That bells should joyful ring to tell
A should had gone to heaven; ....[36]

The poem above points out the ironic situation in announcing the death of a person by tolling the bell. People take it as a mark of mourning, though the tolling of the bell, according to her, should be associated with the announcement of the happy news. Then she asks rhetorically if the time of death with grief indicates that heaven is sad at the arrival of a soul. She, therefore, considers the tolling to be "joyful ring" announcing the soul's arrival in heaven. The following four-lined poem of Emily Dickinson expresses that the idea or the thought of death should not puzzle us because it is stark reality of life and generations have died-

> That such have died enable us
> The tranquiller to die:
> That such have lived, certificate
> For immortality.[37]

She reminds us of the fact that we are living and the generations are born one after another. This shows that there is some unknown power that controls death and that there is some unknown region too, from where we come trailing the glory of that region. She conceives of the Earth as a kindly - fond mother for human beings, who lay them to eternal slumber after their life-long toil.

Thus to Emily Dickinson's inquisitive and sensitive mind, immortality was indeed a "colossal substance" which she could not hope to grasp without persistent efforts of her alert mind. But finally she conquered her doubts and climbed out of the depths of her skepticism to walk in the sunshine of her belief and to sing in inimitable voice of radiant joy :

> I live with Him - I hear His voice
> I stand alive - Today -[38]

Thus:

> The Earth lays back there tired lives
> In her mysterious Drawers -
> Too tenderly that any doubt
> An ultimate Repose -
> The manner of the children -
> Who weary of the Day -

Themself ? - the noisy plaything
They cannot put away -[39]

The imagery of tired children at play, even in the evening, unwilling to give up their play until they are gently weaned away by their mother, has been very effectively employed to convey the benign act on the part of the Earth.

REFERENCES

1. Thomas H. Johnson (ed.), *The Complete Poems of Emily Dickinson*, (Delhi, Kalyani Publishers, 1960), Poem No. 1499, p. 631.
2. *Ibid.*, Poem No. 696, p. 343.
3. *Ibid.*, Poem No. 1012, pp. 467-468.
4. *Op. cit.*, Poem No. 1205, p. 532.
5. *Ibid.*, Poem No. 79, p. 41.
6. *Idem.*
7. *Ibid.*, Poem No. 1162, p. 518.
8. *Op. cit.*, Poem No. 1234, p. 542.
9. *Ibid.*, Poem No. 306, p. 144.
10. Thomas H. Johnson, *Emily Dickinson: An Interpretative Biography* (U.S.A., Harvard University Press, 1967), p. 233.
11. *Idem.*
12. *Idem.*
13. Johnson, *The Complete Poems*, Poem No. 1021, p. 470.
14. Johnson, *Interpretative Biography*, pp. 234-235.
15. Johnson, *op. cit.*, Poem No. 1545, p. 644.
16. *Ibid.*, Poem No. 501, p. 243.
17. *Idem.*
18. Johnson, *Biography*, p. 241.
19. *Idem.*
20. Johnson, *The Complete Poems*, Poem No. 1461, p. 619.
21. *Ibid.*, Poem No. 413, p. 197.
22. *Idid.*, Poem No. 376, p. 179.
23. *Ibid.*, Poem No. 61, p. 32.
24. *Ibid.*, Poem No. 251, p. 115.
25. *Ibid.*, Poem No. 721, pp. 353-354.
26. *Idem.*

27. Johnson, *Biography*, pp. 257-258.
28. Johnson, *Complete Works*, Poem No. 1487, p. 627.
29. *Ibid.*, Poem No. 1743, p. 706.
30. *Ibid.*, Poem No. 431, p. 207.
31. *Ibid.*, Poem No. 1205, p. 532.
32. *Ibid.*, Poem No. 827, p. 401.
33. *Ibid.*, Poem No. 974, pp. 455-56.
34. *Ibid.*, Poem No. 420, p. 201.
35. *Ibid.*, Poem No. 705, p. 347.
36. Martha Dickinson Bianchi and Alfred Leete Hampson (eds.) *Poems by Emily Dickinson* (Little Brown and Co. V.S.P., 1952), p. 211.
37. *Ibid.*, p. 198.
38. Johnson, *Complete Poems*, Poem No. 463, pp. 222-223.
39. *Ibid.*, Poem No. 423, p. 202.

STYLE AND TECHNIQUE

6

A word is dead, when it is said
some say -
I say it just begin to live
That day.[1]

Emily Dickinson first sent some of her poems to Higginson for his opinion. She asked whether her poetry was "alive" and whether it "breathed". Indeed she was able to develop a style which made her poems breath. In one of her poems she wrote :

A word that breathes distinctly
Has not the power to die.[2]

Miss Dickinson approached language like an explorer of new lands. She has used words with a creator's licence, coining with the free hand; boldly manoeuvering her inherited vocabulary, collaps the syntax, springing the rhythm, slanding the rhyme. She was a bold experimenter with words. She wrought miracles with language. She has also rearranged word-order to secure emphasis and surprise. There is the device of shifting grammatical categories, for example "pomp" as an adjective and "create" as a participle.

There is hardly a line of Emily's work, however, which fails to throw out some gleam of genuine original power of imagination and of real emotional thought. There is the real poetic motive here. The high music has been with her always. There is centainly rude and half barbaric naivety in many of the poems. They show the insight of the civilized adult combined with the simplicity of savage child :

Angles in the early morning
May be seen the dews among

Stopping, plucking, smiting, flying
Do the birds to them belong?[3]

. . . . .

Is not this the voice of a child? The irregularity of form does not mar the depth and originality of ethical themes.

Pain has an element of blank:
It cannot recollect
When it began, or if there were
A day when it was not.[4]

Here is genuine, emotional insight into life, united with no small power of feeling.

It would be pertinent now to make some observations, on the poetic idiom and the manner of expression employed by Emily Dickinson. It would not be an exaggeration to remark that she was more or less an unlettered poet, since she does not seem to have cultivated her art through an assiduous erudition. She may have casually and curiously read some English classics in the school or at home but we have no evidence to show that she was as learned as John Keats in the poetical lore. Thus Emily Dickinson was entirely an original poet, who followed no literary tradition or poetical style. She fashioned her own poetic idiom through her limited experience and crystalized her style through her own experiments without the advantage of a mentor.

The frontiers of her experience and knowledge lay within a narrow locality of Amherst and a few friends and relations. She evinced no interest in the political affairs of the country and the Civil War that wrecked the whole nation, left her unruffled and undisturbed. Only the Transcendental and Unitarian Movements spear-headed by Emerson and other Boston Brahmins engaged her attention and shaped her views on religion. But the literary trends of the day had no influence on her. Beginning with Valentine and Snatches of verses scribbled on pieces of waste-paper or used envelope, she ascended to the Parnassian height with the help of her own, unschooled artistic sensibilities. She developed her manner of expression by relying upon the limited range of experience and daily-intercourse, picking symbols provided by what she could see through the window of her room; or by the surroundings of her home. The sun, the moon, the horizon, the lightning, the funeral procession, the basket, which she often used to pull up things from below, the ripe corn in the fields, the row of graves in the church-yard, these constitute the repertory of the images and symbols which she frequently employs.

The result is a startling innovation in the poetic style which not only at once engages our attention and absorbs our interest but also leads to an immediacy of experience. If she uses the traditional symbols, she refurnishes and reinforces them with novel, semantic and metaphorical connotations, she says-

A long, long sleep, a famous sleep
That makes no show for dawn.[5]

Likewise, she employs words in a startlingly new sense, sometimes using their obsolete meaning or imparting to them an extended meaning. Her vocabulary is small and limited but these limitations she turns to a happy account by an austerior use of words. Like Jane Austen she too works on a two inch ivory and works wonders on it, confining herself within the four-walls of the room, she led an intense inner life with her thoughts and musings acquiring a marked introversion. This way of living made her imaginative life richer, more daring and made in tune with the unknown, unfathomed mysteries of the life and the world beyond it. With her spiritual insight thus rendered inner and her institutions more powerful, Emily Dickinson could see behind the veil of phenomena and could express what she saw there in a highly condensed style. In a mood of intense strong experience, she dispenses with auxiliary words freely using ellipses, dashes and interjections and capital letters to convey the whole gamut of her emotion, in the fewest possible words e.g. the use of dashes in a single line-

Just so -Jesus- raps-He-doesn't weary-[6]

Emily Dickinson is extremely fond of using capital letters.

Wild Nights - wild Nights
were I with thee
Futile - the winds-
To a heart in port-[7]

Her style and poetic diction, to quote the famous words of Bacon, are "imitating none and immitable by any". The adage that the "style is the man" is very apt to her technique since it mirrors her unique poetical character and inner self.

Emily Dickinson's chief characteristics are: a faculty for seizing the impression or feeling of the movement and fixing them with rare force and accuracy, and a vividness of imagery which impresses the reader as thoroughly unconventional and shows considerable imaginative power. The following quotation is a fair specimen of some of the most striking poems written by Emily Dickinson :

Exultation is the going
of an inland soul to sea,
Past the house - past the headlands-
Into deep Eternity.[8]

There is a curious energy in the tone and words. Indeed it is the tone rather than the words that one remembers afterwards. Her tone is wholly spontaneous. There is no literary assumption of posture or pose in advance.

Emily Dickinson is already in the poem before she begins it, as a child is already in the adventure before he finds a word to speak of it. The punctuation may bewilder us. The density of the thing said may defeat our understanding. But one will read on nevertheless because he will not be able to stop. Something is being said to us and we have no choice but hear.

Imagery and rhythm are not the only bricks of poetic structure. Emily's poems are made of nothing but words. She has a passion for words, we know both from her poems and from her own confession. She has a little harbour full of frequently voyaging words any one of which would now be regarded as leaking enough to sink on ordinary lyric. Her poems somehow support the words; she is able to persuade us to read them not as worn-out generalizations, but as fresh expressions. But in spite of this paradoxical triumph, no one, would condemn that Emily's words explain Emily. It is the voice rather than the form which supplies the key to her words. This voice not only speaks but speaks to you. The subject of poetry is the human experience and its object must therefore be humanity, even in a time like ours when humanity seems to prefer to limit its knowledge of the experience of life, to the life the advertisers offer it. It is no excuse to a poet that humanity will not listen. The unforgettable lore does not clamour at us even when its words are the words of passion or of agony. This is a New England voice—it belongs to a woman who "sees new Englandly". There is a poem of Emily Dickinson which none of us can read unmoved—which infact moves very deeply:

I can wade grief -
Whole Pools of it -
I'm used to that -
But the least push of Joy
Break up my feet-[9]

Emily Dickinson is not only the actor in this poem, she is the observer of the action also. When we are drawn in 'Self-pity' we throw ourselves into ourselves and go down. But Emily is both in and out of it, both suffers and sees it, which is to say that she is a poet.

The reader of Emily Dickinson's poems will feel that without her extraordinary mastery of tone her achievement would have been impossible. To write constantly of death, of grief, of despair, of agony, of fear is almost to ensure the failure of art, for these emotions overwhelm the mind and art must surmount experience to master it. A morbid art is an imperfect art.

There was never a more delicate dancing on the crumbling edge of the abyss of Self-pity that suicidal temptation of the lonely - that Emily Dickinson's but she rarely tumbles in. She sees herself in the awkward stumbling attitude and laughs.

The following four lines were written probably on the third anniversary of Emily's father's death. It is one of her greater poems and perhaps the only poem she ever wrote which carries the curious and solemn weight of perfection:

Lay this laurel on the one
Too intrinsic for Renown
Laurel - veil your deathless tree-
Him you chasten, that is He![10]

Another important quality of the poetry of Emily Dickinson which fascinates and sometimes baffles the reader is the skilful use of irony :

Superiority to Fate
Is difficult to gain
'Tis not conferred of Any
But possible to earn.[11]

or

I many times thought Peace had come when Peace was far away-[12]

or

The First Day's Night had come-
And grateful that a thing
So terrible - had been endured
I told my soul to sing-[13]

Such poems show that human experience is capricious and untrustworthy that it is characterized by crucial ambiguities, by an unremitting mysteriousness, and by an appealing lack of the predictable or the certain. Peace when it seems near enough, suddenly becomes a delusion, suffering is somehow a price we are compelled to pay for ecstasy. Agony recedes but after a brief respite, emerges again with devastating consequences. Nothing is dependable. All values are unreliable.

Irony as an attitude towards life, represents to Emily Dickinson the sort of steadfast composure which declines involvements.

The sun - just touched the Morning-
The Morning - happy thing -
supposed that he had come to dwell
And Life would all the spring !

The Morning-fluttered - staggered
Felt feebly - for Her crown
Her unannointed forehead
Henceforth - Her only one ![14]

Morning assumed that her ecstasy would be permanent; she actively depended on the sun.

In Emily Dickinson's view, man is the absolute pawn of circumstance. There is no sense in which it can be said of the individual that he has made things happen. Rather he is portrayed as the massive observer, who can merely look on, while things happen to him. Weighing man against the gigantic forces that control his destiny, Emily Dickinson does necessarily see him as at once paltry and trivial.

In Emily Dickinson's poetry, thus, irony functions as a constant and pervasive theme and inevitably the ironic outlook came to affect Miss Dickinson's poetic style, to influence not just what she said but also her manner of expression. What we initially took for straight lines - the easy movements from dark to light from fear to peace - becomes circles as the poem returns us to the very states which it appeared to have abolished. Therein lies the fineness of Emily Dickinson's ironic style.

We must accept the style of Emily Dickinson as we accept her themes, seeing that her work style is the measure of content and that both were of prime importance to the way of life Emily Dickinson adopted.

To explore some of Dickinson's Poetic Stylistic technicalities, reference can me made to a very famous poem of Emily 'Because I could not stop for Death' as a model poem. It includes some glimpses of the poetess, death as an obsession with Dickinson, the poem, the character of her verse which emphasizes brevity, compactness and compression, choice of words, the technique of obscurity, capitalization of words, the cryptic use of dashes, the rhyme scheme, Imagery Symbolism and the use of metaphors. This poem leaves an indelible effect upon the reader's mind. Death here acquires a new dimension. It is portrayed as a restful trip, a pleasant journey with a courteous visitor and an unnoticed third travelles – Immortality.

Death can be interpreted as an escort to the victim, to a new state of existence or it may be considered as a deceiver to lead the victim to the poem of destruction. No doubt, the poem leaves the question of the final destiny open for the readers to decide; and it is remarkable for its mundane subject and a complex but unique poetic style.

Because I could not stop for Death –
He kindhy stopped for me –
The carriage held but just Ourselves –
And Immortality.
We slowly drove – He knew no haste
And I had put away
My labour and my leisure too,
For His Civility –
We passed the School, Where children strove
At Recess – in the Ring –
We passed the Fields of Gazing Grain –
We passed the Setting Sun –
Or rather – He passed Us –
The Dews drew quivering and chill –
For only Gossamer, my Gown –
My Tippet – Only Tulle –
We paused before a House that Seemed
A swelling of the Ground –
The Roof was scarcely visible –
The Cornice – in the Ground –
Since then – His Centuries – and yet
Feels shorter than the Day
I first Surmised the Horses' heads
Were toward Eternity –

Here we find that Emily evolved a way of her own with words. She coined and created new words. Skillfully manicuring them to suit her purpose, thus collapsing the syntax, springing the rhythm and slanting the rhymes. Words sprang as it were from the inner fountains of her heart and she gradually discovered her poetic powers through the miracles of language.

Her verse is steeped in mysticism and often packed with cryptic meaning and is unmelodious in expression. The main ingredients of her style which characterize her verse are brevity, compactness, conciseness, the use of bold and original words, employment of paradoxes, riddles, irony, ambiguity, epigrams, epithets, hyperboles and aphorisms. Her technique of obscurity, vivid imagery, concrete and novel metaphors and symbols, the element of surprise along with the above ingredients – all have helped to charge her style with life.

This particular poem has short stanzas, mostly quatrains. An awesome reality like 'death' is described with utmost simplicity frugality and economy of words. Death comes in as a kindly gentleman, skillfully wooing the mistress away for a joyful ride. The lady readily agrees to go with him. In other words, the protagonist triumphs over death by accepting it with civility and calm. It is a simple yet mysterious poem for it talks of 'death-in-life' and a sense of reconciliation. The poem runs into six stanzas. The first three stanzas talk about earthly activities, the mystery of work and joy and temporal time. The last two stanzas mark a definite transition from the mortal world to the immortal one, from the material one to an assurance of eternal life. The cosmic jostles the everyday and is illumined by 'eternity' which is live an unexpected guest. The fourth stanza, which used to be omitted in the past by a few editors, is a slight detachment from the main theme.

Compression, aphorism and epigrammatically are Dickinson's tools with which she proceeds. Without any preparation or apology. She takes the reader by surprise by her abrupt beginnings and by the sharp sudden zigzags. The first two lines of the poem directly condense the theme of death. The mere mention of the word brings before the mind ideas associated with death, i.e. the transitory existence of the material world, terror of the grave, the presumptions of an after life. All these ideas have been wonderfully packaged with the utmost brevity and conciseness and rendered with an artistic perfection. Her poetic genius is embedded in the scrumptious choice of words she makes to express both surface and deep-rooted meanings. On the surface, the poem may appear live a lover taking his mistress out for a joy ride or it may be a simple funeral procession to the grave. But metaphorically, it denotes deeper levels of meaning - a spiritual journey of a different wind. Death comes like a kindly gentleman in a 'carriage' (which is nothing but a hearse) allowing her to snaton away some moments from 'labour and leisure' (the daily chokes of earthly life) to take her for a ride (the funeral procession) through the outlying country, passing 'children' at school, the 'gazing grain', 'the Setting Sun' moving beyond the open country to a new 'house' (the grove). The undercurrents of awe and terror accompanying death are subdues by the word 'civility' of the driver (death) who is merely driving has towards the ultimate house. The tomb to prepare her for a life beyond it, i.e. 'immortality'. As she herself was too occupied with life and since she could not stop for death, it kindly stopped for death.

Besides the ardent use of words, another most striking signature of Dickinson's style is her technique of obscurity. Every one of her phrases and her changing rhythm is a direct reflection of her complex personality and her varying poetic moods. This poem is a gradual progression from a self-pleasured, comfortable, busty life of a mortal to a full realization of the ultimate purpose of death, an escort leading one to the threshold of immortality. We find that a sudden climax is reached in the word 'eternity'. The word conveys beautifully the chill finality of death. Her technique though obscure is an impressive revelation of her poetic attitude which registers her spiritual experiences.

Another unmistakable personal stamp which makes her poems obscure is the capitalization of words and the cryptic use of dashes. In all her poems, Dickinson capitalized key words like nouns, adjectives, verbs and even adverbs. This may be for emphasis or to confer a new dignity to the words. It consists of fifty-seven capitals in all, with twenty-four capitals at the beginning of lines and thirty-three capitals, twenty-seven are nouns, two are adjectives, six are pronouns, five conjunctions, two articles and two verbs. The capitalization of all line nouns like Death, Carriage, Immortality, School, etc. is charged with a significant connotation, and conveys an important message. The poem even has capitalised pronouns like he, we, my, ourselves, us. 'He' signifies death which 'occupies' a prominent place in the poem and since 'death' comes in like a visitor, a friend, a gentleman, he demands a dignified position. 'We', 'Ourselves', and 'V's' again represent the three pivotal characters in the poem, viz. the victim, death and immortality. The use of capitals for other words like Or, Feels, Were, At, etc. incorporate with her style of starting every fresh line with a capital letter that her lyrics are highly subjective, personal and autobiographical becomes evident from the use of the first person singular pronoun 'I', for she knew no other consciousness. Although she asserted that the 'I' in her poems was a fictitious person, in most cases her poetry was largely confessional about her own inner self. The deployment of 'I' in the present poem clearly reflects Dickinson's obsession with death and life after death.

Besides capitalization, the complexity of her style reaches its Zenith by her capricious use of 'dashes', instead of punctuations marks. The over-abundant use of dashes, confuses and baffles the reader. The 'dash' is almost an exclusive mark of punctuation in her poems. But it affects the meaning and tone of the poems. It becomes difficult to decide when these dashes indicate a comma, a semi-colon, a full-stop, a metrical pause or a pause of anticipation or suspense. Critics have termed them as 'stylistic irregularities' which often justify her eccentricity and amateurishness.

There are altogether twenty-two dashes in the entire poem. In stanza One, the dash after 'death' indicates a comma. The pause is necessary to introduce the civility of the visitor. The one after 'me' indicate a full stop. Initially the carriage held just the two of them and an unnoticed third travelles – Immortality, which is an indication that the soul is just making a departure from the body on to a long pilgrimage into eternity.

In stanza two, the dash between 'we drove slowly' and 'he knew no haste' stands for a semi-colon, to separate the two main clauses. Semi-colon, to separate the two main clauses. In stanza three, the dash after 'recess' stands for a comma separating two phrases – 'at recess' and 'in the ring'. The pause between the two becomes necessary to show that although the children one giving full vent to their childish emotions during the school break, yet they are confined only within the boundaries of the school, i.e. 'in the ring'. Again the 'dash' after 'ring' stands for a full-stop for it marks the finality of the idea and makes way for another to begin. The dash after 'gazing grain' again stands for a semi-colon for on the surface it separates two main clauses but figuratively presents two contrasting ideas of maturity and decline of bright sunshine and duke of life. The dash after 'the Setting Sun' and 'or rather' in stanza four is appropriate in its place for what follows after both is a reformulating phrase. The dash after 'chill' may seem to make a pause of anticipation, symbolizing the chill of death and foreseeing the scantiness of dress. The dashes which separate 'gown', 'Tippet', and 'Tulle' could be used to highlight the key-phrases in order to create an emphatic effect. These key phrases were not the usual burial clothes but those meant for a bride. In stanza five the dash after the phrase 'A Swelling of the Ground', stands for a semi-colon, to indicate an anticipating pause. It is however difficult to offer any substantial explanation of the use of these capricious dashes. Perhaps they were meant to make sharp clauses and phrases fall into their logical places, or to produce an overall effect through her pauses, or to break away from the traditional pattern of syntax.

Besides the eccentric punctuation, Dickinson's poems are also marked by her erratic rhymes and rhythms. A large number of her rhymes appear to be somewhat partial, slant or are termed as 'off rhymes'. Yet others are so feeble that they are hardly recognizable. Her rhymes were greatly influenced by the biblical hymns she heard in her childhood. The irregularity in her rhymes can be explained through her relief that any mechanical regularity always created monotony, and she felt no real compulsion to use exact rhymes. We therefore find in her poems a variety of Scattered rhymes ranging from exact rhymes and eye rhymes to identical rhymes, vowel rhymes, imperfect rhymes and suspended rhymes. In this poem the rhyming pattern seems to be very vague, varied and absolutely irregular. At times the rhymes are alternate, at times they occur in two consecutive lines — one following the other. There is one identical and one vowel rhyme used alternately in stanza one and five :

e.g. me / mi:/ and immortality / im : t re l a ti / [vowel rhyme]
ground / ground / and ground / graund / [identical rhyme]
Stanzas 1, 2 and 6 have imperfect rhymes which alternate in stanzas 1 and 6 and follow each other in Stanza 2. These rhymes consist of the same vowel sounds followed by different consonants there we find that there is hardly any harmony between content and form. One also observes that live has rhymes she also loosened the set traditional metres to evade monotony. A metrical analysis of the poem shows that the poem partly follows the iambic tetrameter pattern, and partly the trimester pattern.

This poem is replete with images and symbols. Abstract ideas like 'death' and 'immortality' are personified and dramatized, highlighted and placed in exciting relation with one another. Death here is personified. Instead of the awesome terrifying experience associated with death, she has created an image of death as a person, a family friend or a lover, who with his gracious manners woos the lady away.

There is also a third unnoticed traveler 'Immortality' - a symbol of the soul departing from the body and travelling to a new existence. Death is a harsh reality which waits for no man. It lays its icy hands on mortals and carries them away to an unknown world. But Dickinson here has minimized death's sensational aspects. She has very skillfully handed the effects of death's unexpected visit upon the victim. The poem slowly progressed from a cheerful, comfortable anticipation to gradual fear and doubt about death's deception and terrifying motives. A whole range of earthly life is presented by exquisite images of children playing in school, the swaying grain, gazing away as if waiting to be harvested, and the amber glow of the setting sun. All these natural sights symbolize the three stages of youth, maturity and age. They also present the earthly cycles of rotation (causing day and night) and revolution (cycle of seasons).

Every image in the poem is carefully pointed to convey an extended meaning. Dickinson has combined the celestial betrothal with a metaphor of a 'funeral' as the wedding journey to 'eternity'. Her chief source of inspiration for presenting such a typically Christian theme was the 'Bible'. As the journey comes to an end, death slowly recedes into the background and in the last stanza the perspective changes. Death breaks off all connections and there is a sudden change from the limited earthly existence to a new dimension of limitless time - a new state of existence, 'Eternity'. It is centuries since the body is deposited and yet the centuries seem shorten than the first day when she experienced the sun-set of her life - the awful power and shock of death.

Like Donne, she was inordinately fond of the paradox, which she used to express the fundamental disharmonies of life. The following are some of her famous paradoxical utterances:

Success is counted sweetest
By those who never succeed.[15]

And-

A wounded Deer-leaps highest-
I've heard the Hunter tell-[16]
x x x x

or

To learn the transport - by the Pain
As Blind Man learns the sun ![17]
x x x x
Just lost when I was saved !

or

Just felt the world go by ![18]
x x x x
We lose-because we win[19]

The ideas stated in above extracts of Emily Dickinson's poems are basically tragic. She likewise remains aloof from the sentimental truism—"success in failure" or "sweet are the uses of Adversity".

Yet another technical excellency which Emily may be said to have exploited is a kind of cryptic economy of statements and, since economy is always conducive to poetic expression, a poetic quality is sometimes achieved. Perhaps the following example will illustrate the meaning :

> Title divine - is mine !
> The wife-without the sign
> Acute Degree-Conferred on me-
> Empress of Calvary![20]

One can suck wisdom from her compact writings. Emily Dickinson uses the demonstrative pronouns "it" in reference to a friend of hers:

> If I may have 'it' when 'it' is dead
> I will contented be:
> If just as soon as breath is out
> 'It' shall belong to me'[21]

The unique use of 'it' in reference to a human-being reminds us of Miranda's speech in Shakespeare's 'The Tempest' where she exclaims :

> 'Why is't? a spirit ?
> Lord, how it looks about believe me, Sir,
> It carries a brave form: but 'tis a spirit.'

Emily is very fond of using, metaphors, and personifications. In many poems, Death has been described, having a distinct personality, performing various roles.

> Because I could not stop for Death
> He kindly stopped for me;
> The carriage held but just ourselves
> And Immortality.[22]

She also uses euphemism when she writes—

> Death is a dialogue between
> The Spirit and the Dust
> "Dissolve" says Death-The Spirit "Sir
> I have another Trust"[23]

From ellipses to crystalized images was not a far cry and Emily Dickinson thus enjoys the pride of place as the fore-runner of Ezra Found and his followers.

Emily was an imagist par-excellence, before imagism was born. In the white-heat of emotions she could create through her concentrated power of imagination and her introspective fervour, crystalized images. The following poem can serve as an apt example —

> The grave my little cottage is,
> Where, keeping house for thee,
> I make my parlor orderly
> And lay the morble tea,
> For two divided, briefly
> A cycle, it may be,
> Till everlasting life unit-
> In strong society.[24]

The above poem presents a number of clear images, e.g. the image of grave as a cottage, as a parlour the image of the cycle of birth and death; the image of a strong society, i.e. the heavenly abode. Another fine example of imagery can be taken from the following extract of her poem:

> The corn her furthest kernel filled
> Before the coming frail
> When there leaned into perfectness
> Through haze of burial.[25]

The above poem presents a very distinct image of the ripe grain fields, just ready to be sifted. Similarly, there is the image of a man, just died, whose soul has to be separated from his mortal body.

As has been pointed out by the critics, there is a close affinity between the seventeenth century metaphysical poets and Emily Dickinson. It is chiefly the poems on Death and Immortality that highlight this affinity. Henry Vaughan's poem entitled as "Reverie" dwells upon the soul's return to heaven just as Emily's poem visualizes the colossal substance of Immortality. In both the poets, we find, the thought melting into emotion. Thus in both Vaughan and Emily Dickinson, an idea attains the level of poetic perfection. Wordsworth famous 'Ode on Immortality' is a poetic argument, an answer to a spiritual questioning, worked out through ratiocination in a poetic frame-work. Hence it lacks the initial insight which reveals a truth in a flash of enlightenment. Emily's poetry, on the colossal substance of Immortality, is aesthetically and artistically more satisfying than that of Vaughan's because of the immediacy and force of its effect upon our imagination.

We find in Emily Dickinson's poems, an association of sensibility with intellect, of thought with emotion, of imagination with reason, such as we come across in the best poems of John Donne.

Emily Dickinson does not affect metaphysics but the metaphysical ideas and conceits come to her naturally as leaves to a tree - hence her poetry is free from the tedious mannerism. Literary conventions did not exist for her, as a poet she was quite untroubled by public opinion. Everything in her work is immediate, personal, original and honest. Many of Emily Dickinson's letters are caskets of jewels. There are phrases that are poems in epitome. Her thought is clothed itself in the essential graces of poetic simplicity and music.

The poems of Emily Dickinson must be seen whole in the sky and must be touched to yield their lightning. Martha Hale Shackford, describing the essential characteristics of Emily Dickinson's poetry, rightly observes that idea and expression are so indissolubly fused in her work that no analysis of her style can be attempted without realizing that everyone of her phrases, her changing rhythm is a direct reflection of her own personality. Her works show an intensity of spiritual experience. They are in fact a record of a soul endowed with unceasing activity in a world, not material, but one where concrete facts are the cherished revelation of divine significances. But Emily Dickinson's poetic style and technique also suffer from severe criticism and limitations. Ella Gilbert Iver has gone to the extent of saying that she has not dwelt upon Emily Dickinson's faults; they speak for themselves and sometimes with such a din that the virtues cannot be heard. Granted that her poetry is uneven, so rugged of rhyme and rhythm that it jolts the mind like a crowdy road - she prefers it to a flowery bed of ease. Many can lull, but few can awake. Departure from literary usage, faulty grammar and syntax, illegitimate word-formation and false rhymes are some other oddities of Dickinson's style.

Emily's meter at its worst is a kind of stiff sing-song, her diction at its worst is a kind of poetic nursery-jargons. Her incoherence and formlessness are fatal.

Herbert Read observes in one of his articles titled "The Range of Emily Dickinson":

> I was surprised at the actual number of the poems—Many of them very short, four or six lines only .... It is the sameness that amounts to poverty of technique. It would not be unfair to compare these small poems with the works of a painter who had all his life painted small pictures of similar subject in one colour, with one texture ....[26]

The justification for the host of linguistic and stylistic charges is that she creates her own technique and moulds language to the requirements of her personal voice without regard to any set conventions. In other words she was a self-conscious rebel with a direct style. Duncan concludes that Dickinson's art was the product of a privately trained instinct. She is without any pretenses of intellectualism. But she used the related skills of analysis, criticism, definition and argument.

Besides she used many aphorisms and paradoxes. She had Romantic faith in the imagination and Puritan, classical distrust of it. Her language combines reason and strange logic.

Emily Dickinson paradoxically achieves the highest art of the artlessness of her method. Living amid the velvet hush of American Victorianism, she blew clarion notes of the shocking truth, a daughter of Puritanism she pushed past the rigid image of fear and took her God confidentially by the hand and ludicrous far-fetchedness of the seventeenth-century metaphysical poets.

Hence, Emily Dickinson's genius was as erratic as it was brilliant. Her disregard for accepted forms or for regularities was incorrigible. Grammar, rhymes, metre, anything went by the board if it stood in the way of thought or freedom of utterance. As her experiences are quite complex, she is not moved by any traditional metrical form and her experiments are bold and innovating.

Her works have had considerable influence on modern poetry. Her frequent use of dashes, sporadic capitalization of nouns, off-rhymes, broken metre, unconventional metaphors have contributed her reputation as one of the most innovative poets of the 19th century American literature. Amherst has became a pilgrimage for her fans and aspiring lyricists, her life and work has attracted a numbers of scholars, and like Sylvia Plath, her poetry has inspired feminist writers. Dickinson is also one of those poets whose words have given much comfort for people who have mental problems.

> 'Hope is the thing with feathers
> That perches in the soul,
> And sings the tune without the words
> And never stops at all,
>
> And sweetest in the gale is heard;
> And sore must be the storm
> That could abash the little bird
> That kept so many warm.
>
> I've heard it in the chillest land,
> And on the strangest sea;
> Yet, never, in extremity,
> It asked a crumb of one'.[27]

Later feminist critic have challenged the popular conception of the poet as reclusive, eccentric figure, and underlined her intellectual struggle and passive aggressiveness. Her verse is full of allusions to volcanoes, shipwrecks, funerals, and other manifestations of natural and human voilence, which she hide into her writings. Because of her frequent use of common metre, many of Dickinson's poems can easily be set to tunes (for example 'I heard a fly buzz when I died - The Stillness in the Room/Was like the Stillness in the Air/Between the Heaves of Storm'). Dickinson's poetry has been used as texts for art songs by composers such as Aaron Copland, and Nick Perus. Because of this, one can also sing many of her poems to the tunes of 'Amazing Grace', 'The Yellow Rose of Texas', or the 'Gilligan's Island' theme song. While this novelty is entertaining in itself, it also demonstrates the connection between poetry and song embodied for centuries in the ballad.

References

1. Thomas H. Johnson (ed.), *The Complete Poems of Emily Dickinson.* (Delhi, Kalyani Publishers, 1960), Poem No. 1212, pp. 534-535.
2. *Ibid.*, Poem No. 1651, pp. 675-676.
3. *Ibid.*, Poem No. 94, p. 47.
4. *Ibid.*, Poem No. 650, pp. 323-324.
5. *Ibid.*, Poem No. 654, p. 326.
6. *Ibid.*, Poem No. 317, pp. 149-150.
7. *Op. cit.,* Poem No. 249, p. 114.
8. *Ibid.*, Poem No. 76, p. 39.
9. *Ibid.*, Poem No. 252, p. 115.
10. *Ibid.*, Poem No. 1393, p. 597.
11. *Ibid.*, Poem No. 1081, p. 490.
12. *Op. cit.*, Poem No. 739, p. 362.
13. *Op. cit.*, Poem No. 410, p. 195.
14. *Ibid.*, Poem No. 232, p. 106.
15. *Ibid.*, Poem No. 67, p. 35.
16. *Ibid.*, Poem No. 165, p. 77.
17. *Ibid.*, Poem No. 167, p. 79.
18. *Op. cit.*, Poem No. 160, p. 75.
19. *Op. cit.*, Poem No. 21, p. 15.
20. *Op. cit.*, Poem No. 1072, p. 487.
21. *Ibid.*, Poem No. 577, p. 281.
22. *Ibid.*, Poem No. 712, p. 350.
23. *Ibid.*, Poem No. 976, p. 456.
24. *Ibid.*, pp. 706-707.
25. *Ibid.*, Poem No. 962, p. 450.
26. Herbert Read, *The Range of Emily Dickinson,* (Cambridge, 1950).
27. Johnson, *Complete Poems*, Poem No. 77, p. 40.

EMILY DICKINSON'S HORIZONS AND HER SEXUALITY

7

Traditionally, Walt Whitman is considered the bard of vastness, the poet of the American Sublime. Emily Dickinson is seen as his opposite, as having reveled in enclosed spaces, in solitude. Everything about her, except her talent, appears tiny: her sequestered life in her Amherst family home, the petite white dress she wore (now hanging on display there), the scraps of paper she wrote her poems on in minuscule handwriting. Even the verses have short lines—tetrameter or trimeter, as a rule—and rarely extend beyond a stanza or two. "I am small like the wren," she herself coyly informed a correspondent who had not met her. Thus the image most of us gleaned in school of an eccentric if engaging New England spinster who wrote about unrequited love and the beauty of nature, and who was so shy toward strangers that she would not come down to the parlor to meet them, but sat listening to their conversations from atop the staircase or from behind a door.

Over the last few decades, though, a number of feminist critics have chipped away at this picture. Adrienne Rich's volcanic essay "Vesuvius at Home: The Power of Emily Dickinson"; Sharon Cameron's fierce interpretation of the Lyric "My Life had stood—a Loaded Gun," in her essay "The Dialectic of Rage"; Cynthia Griffin Wolff's 1986 biography, portraying a dissident daughter of Calvinism blazing her own theological trails—all these and similar challenges to conventional Dickinson scholarship depict a complicated rebel turning against the rigid roles defined by her society, a colossus defying Victorian patriarchy with her female language and values.

In "The Passion of Emily Dickinson" (Harvard, 390), Judith Farr takes stock of the contradictory views, winnows them, and comes up with yet another perspective. She sees the poet as a complex figure whose largeness defeats attempts to neatly categorize her. The book's epigraph from Emerson's "Nature", alludes to the essential quality the critic perceives in Dickinson's work as this transfiguration which all material objects undergo through the passion of the poet along with poet's inner visions.

Part of Farr's study concentrates on the issue of influence, "the poet's connection with literary or artistic works: her reclusion and self-description as a nun with the nuns of Tennyson and the Pre-Raphaelites, for example; her mysterious emblem of the white dress with scriptural Revelation and [Dante Gabriel] Rossetti's saintly maidens....Even as Dickinson's quotation of mid-Victorian literary texts was wider than has been supposed, she knew far more about 19th century visual art than has generally been thought." In poem after poem, Farr observes, Dickinson connected her writing with the pictorial. Sometimes she called her word-painting "needlework", the most common female art practiced in her day. But often the poems actually refer to painters: Van Dyck, Holman Hunt and, most notably, American Luminists like Frederick Edwin Church or Thomas Cole.

"The Voyage of Life", a tetralogy of canvases painted by Cole, was especially esteemed in New England area. Its sequence depicts an Everyman in infancy, youth, adulthood, and old age, steering a small boat through landscapes that blend exotic foliage and the rugged grandeur of the Adirondack wilderness. In the artist's suggestion that our scenery reflects an Edenic, unfallen nature, Dickinson recognized a perception of the sublime corresponding to the one that she strove to express:

> Perhaps I asked too large—
> I take—no less than skies—
> For Earths, grow thick as
> Berries, in my native town—
> My Basket holds—just Firmaments—
> These—dangle easy—on my arm,
> But smaller bundles—Cram.[1]

The Amherst social life that Emily renounced was, in many respects, more claustrophobic than her narrow room. Her brother, Austin, and sister-in-law, Sue, were convivial and ambitious. Many famous men and women enjoyed the hospitality of their house, "The Evergreens," viewable from the recluse's window. Talk there was often exalted, for Sue was a brilliant, educated woman who craved the company of writers, artists and public figures. Yet the couple was unhappy. Austin conducted a long, unconcealed liaison with Mabel Loomis Todd, the wife of a friend. No wonder Emily felt that "earths" (taken as worldly preoccupations) choked out her breathing space, or that she sought the freedom of airier mental vistas. Farr argues persuasively that Emily's preference for timelessness and a grand scale over temporal pettiness fueled her attraction to the contemplative nun's role. She identified herself with the vestal by wearing white, the color of novices, and by wedding her virginity to solitude, instead of turning to the conventional marriage chosen by her beloved Sue.

Still, Farr does not hesitate to acknowledge that the poet was motivated by something more than her aesthetic need. In two crucial middle chapters the author addresses a pair of enduring mysteries in Dickinson scholarship: whether an unhappy love affair prompted Emily's withdrawal from society, and the identity of "Master," to whom she wrote three passionate letters and a series of ecstatic verses. It is undeniable that Sue, her close friend since their school days, was the recipient of many ardent poems and missives, and that her waspishness often wounded those who loved her. Biographers have long speculated on the nature of the relationship between the two. Farr believes that Sue was, in fact, Emily's muse, as well as one of her two great passions. Recent feminist analyses have cut through the old rationalization that Victorian women habitually addressed friends with endearments we misread as lesbian effusions. The letters and verses clearly express erotic feeling. Sue, however, disliked sex, and though she courted admiration, gave little in return. All three Dickinson siblings learned the high cost of loving her. The pain stung Austin into infidelity, Lavinia into bitterness, and Emily into poetry.

Among the frequenters of Sue's parties was a handsome editor with considerable charismatic charm, especially in the company of women. Samuel Bowles soon became an intimate of the entire Dickinson clan. Amherst gossip linked his name with Sue's, since she often entertained him alone. But he was also one of the small number of people Emily received, and the first to publish any of her verse while she was alive. Farr claims he was the "Master" addressed in the passionate letters (preserved in drafts), and in such erotically charged poems as "Wild nights," "A wife at daybreak I shall be," and "He touched me, so I live to know."

The married but susceptible Bowles is only one of the candidates who have been advanced for the honor. Yet by cracking some of the poet's private literary iconography, Farr makes the strongest case for him. The critic notes that just as Emily linked Sue with Shakespeare's Antony and Cleopatra and Tennyson's Maud, so she associated Bowles, who adored the novels of Charlotte Bronte, with Rochester of Jane Eyre and Lucy Snowe's "Cher Maitre" in Villette. The dates of the Master cycle seem to correspond with known episodes in Bowles' life, moreover, as well as his contact with the Dickinson family. It further appears that the overwrought Emily told him of her troubles with Sue—which the poems suggest marked the onset of mutual love between poet and editor.

The scenario, of course, has its problems. If Dickinson actually engaged in a love affair with Bowles, she must have shared him with several women, including his wife, with whom she corresponded even after his premature death. In addition, one of the strong arguments that "Master" is a fiction of Emily's is that she wrote many fervid poems to her sister-in-law at the same time. Is it credible that she simultaneously loved a man and a woman? Farr is convinced that the idea—dubious to many in the 20th century—would have struck the poet as natural. After all, Shakespeare was her model, and his sonnets, addressed in erotic terms to both a fair man and a treacherous dark lady, were her favourite poems.

SEXUALITY

The Sexuality of Emily Dickinson is a topic of dispute. It has been argued that she may have been bisexual or a lesbian. They are not sure about her preference in sex.

Dickinson's possible romantic and sexual adventures are matters of great controversy among her biographers and critics. There is little evidence on which to base a conclusion about the objects of her affection, though Dickinson's understanding of passion can be inferred through some of her poems and letters.

Attention has focused especially on a group of letters addressed only to "Master", known as the *Master* letters, in which Dickinson appears to be writing to a male lover; neither the addressee of these letters, nor whether they were sent, has been established. Some biographers have been convinced Dickinson might have been romantically involved with the newspaper publisher Samuel Bowles, a friend of her father's, Judge Otis Lord, or a minister named Charles Wadsworth. A relatively recent theory has emerged that proposes William S. Clark, a prominent figure in Amherst at the time, as the identity of her "Master".

Some biographers have theorized Dickinson may have had romantic attachments to women in her younger years, a hypothesis which has grown in popularity. After a claimed romance with Emily Fowler, circa 1850, some conjecture that Susan Gilbert 1851, her closest friend and sister-in-law, was another possible love. The evidence for all these theories is circumstantial at best. Many scholars that claim the evidence for the latter theory about her relationship with women is scant and highly ambiguous.

Peggy Macintosh, from Wellesley College's Center for Research on Women, and Ellen Louise Hart, from University of California at Santa Cruz: Cowell College, in their introduction of Emily Dickinson in *The Heath Anthology of American Literature* (Fifth Edition) note that "It is important to understand the role in Dickinson studies played by homophobia.... We do not know to what extent Dickinson expressed her sexual desires physically...."[2]

Whether Dickinson had romantic feelings for women or not, it is important to remember that her poetry was heavily edited by several people before being released into the public posthumously. According to Macintosh and Hart, there is evidence that Mabel Loomis Todd (the editor) was Austin Dickinson's mistress, and together they "mutilated Dickinson's manuscripts, erasing [Susan's] name and scissoring out references to her." There were lines of poems that were completely scratched out. Todd was involved in the editing of all three initial volumes of Emily's published works. This alteration of documents throws possible romantic aspects into ambiguity.

Other aspects, though, such as their lifelong friendship (late teens to Emily's death), are not ambiguous. It is well-known that no one received more writing from Emily than Susan Gilbert. There were hundreds of letters found, which Gilbert reciprocated. Dickinson's few friendships were all very close, and her friendship with Gilbert was no exception. Some of the letters were very passionate, furthering this ambiguity. While many of Dickinson's letters and poems are highly charged, passionate, and erotic, few biographers or critics believe that Dickinson physically consummated a relationship with anyone.

There is no evidence, in Dickinson's case, that either affair was fully consummated (though Emily and Lavinia were known to indulge in "petting" with suitors). Nevertheless, Farr contends that Emily took the ordinary erotic confusion of her two conflicting relationships and made something epic out of it. Whatever happened, her luminous vision of Eros, depicted on the emotional scale of a Cole painting, has moved readers ever since Mabel Todd and Sue Dickinson began to vie in getting her work published. The 19th century had more than its fair share of Bohemian women writers whose melodramatic lives and loves shipwrecked their artistic discipline. Emily Dickinson, like Charlotte Bronte earlier, recognized that her powerful reactions to stimuli were best channeled into writing when she kept herself sequestered. There passion could not overwhelm her, nor mundane society fritter away her contemplation of eternities.

No doubt other Dickinson scholars will question Farr's readings and identifications. Those who live closely with this poet jealously guard their own understanding of her. But it may be a long time before someone counters with a more carefully reasoned or compelling interpretation. The Passion of Emily Dickinson broadens the horizon of scholarship by adding to our knowledge of the poet's artistic sources. At the same time, it pays elegant tribute to a genius who lived and loved heroically. Dickinson's is the voice of the seas and mountains of the psyche, and, no less than Whitman's, expands the vast landscape of the American Sublime.

REFERENCES

1. Thomas H. Johnson (ed.), *The Complete Poems of Emily Dickinson* (Delhi, Kalyani Publishers, 1960), Poem No. 1221.
2. Pegy Macintosh and E.L. Hart, *The Health Anthology of American Literature* (V edition). http:\\college.hmco.com/english.

8 SUMMING UP

Although Emily Dickinson remained obscure and unknown during her life time yet her first posthumous publications won her remarkable acknowledgement all over the world. Her present eminence is a special triumph, unique in the annals of American letters. She seems to many of us the greatest American poet of the Nineteenth century. Critics do not hesitate to call her poetry wholly derivative, the finest by a woman in the English language.

Emily Dickinson remained a "private" poet all her life. Being unfortunate in her literary advisors and severely limited in her experience of getting her work printed, the choice of remaining a private poet was forced upon her. She felt a deep resentment against what she called the "auction of the mind". Apart from this the term "private poet" has a different sense also, which implies that she believed that poetry could be written only in all-sufficient moments of inspiration. It is clear from the state of her manuscripts. Her verses were set down to satisfy an immediate need; whatever Emily Dickinson's debts to the seventeenth century be, it should never be forgotton that Emerson was the great figure in her foreground and that her conception of poetic language of how the word becomes one with the thing in the moments of inspired vision was basically his.

Emily Dickinson's poems do not belong to the literature of escape. She confronted all the facts of life that came within her experience seeking to record all she could learn; ecstasy or anguish, and stating her conclusions without palliation. Her poems became her absorbing passion, those poems from whose publication she recoiled and which were only made known to the world after her death.

To day, Emily Dickinson is regarded as a major American poet, and the greatest woman-poet in the English language. In spite of her living a secluded life and shutting herself from the main currents of external life, her inward life was so rich with experience that the poetry which is its resultant is a varied aspect. Moreover, her inward experience has been given a most appropriate form of expression, the importance of which is now realized by all critics. She is one of the few instances of a truly dedicated poet and in her life poetry was an all-consuming passion.

The criticism of life which we find in the poems of Emily Dickinson, though apparently disjointly and fragmentary, gives us a clear picture of her most delicate sensitive, and gentle personality, when all the poems are picked together. Each poem provides a glimpse of her central personality and when we have read all of them, there emerges from them a most fascinating, delicately exquisite and a keenly sensitive personality of Emily Dickinson which holds us under its magic spell. While listening to her we lose our personality and prefer to be "nobody" with her.

Life for Emily Dickinson is a vale of sorrow and happiness comes only as a temporary relief. But she accepts it with equanimity and with no complaint. In fact she is so accustomed to suffering, that joy upsets her;

> I can wade grief
> Whole pools of it-
> I'm used to that
> But the least push of joy
> Breaks up my feet ....![1]

Thus, this woman of delicate frame had a courageous heart unafraid of suffering and hardships which are the essential ingredients of life. In this manner the whole of her poetry is a record of her own personal reactions to the various problems connected with Life, Love, Nature, Death and Immortality and in each her approach is fresh and original. For example, about pain, which most of the people think, grows dull with the passage of time, she says-

> They say that "Time Assuages"
> Time never did assuage
> And actual suffering strengthens
> As sinews do, with age.[2]

A life rich within, though outwardly insignificant, is the ideal of Emily Dickinson, and this is exactly the type of life she actually lived. But she does not believe in a passive type of inner life, it has to be lived at white heat, fully responsive to every shade of experience reacting instantaneously to it, and constantly forging itself into a most sensitive and sharp instrument. Living a secluded life, she observed with a keen eye all the natural phenomena around her, and recorded in her poems her most intimate reactions to them. She looked at the flowers, plants and birds with the curiosity of a child and observed minutely their different aspects. In that attitude nature presented herself to her as a playful maiden displaying her beautiful and colourful robes. In the poems of Emily Dickinson, nature appears through two basic moods - as a child's garden of flower, plants and birds, and as a symbol of mysterious process of death. Looking deeper into the process of nature, Emily Dickinson finds that nature is not so gay, innocent and frolicsome as she appears on the surface. At times, she is cold, indifferent and hostile towards man, who feels himself stranger in her midst. Man, therefore, dreads nature's pressure of her inexorable laws which do not spare any one. Who knows that under the attractive designs she hides something terribly destructive.

Commenting on Emily Dickinson's ideas about the relationship of man, Nature, and God, Richard Chase observes in his book "Emily Dickinson", "Generally speaking, Emily Dickinson presented man, nature and God, as radically distinct. She does not share the forms of nineteenth century naturalism which attempts to reconcile the claims of human nature with the claims of cosmic nature .... Nature is both reality and symbol, both house and ghost. The simplicity of nature consists not in its essence but in its function, which is to act as the condition of man's death. We cannot know nature by getting close to it, because the closer we get to nature, the closure we get to unconsciousness and death."

Thus Emily Dickinson believes that there is a mysterious link between nature and man and which cannot be explained by intellect or the scientific method. Thus her poems on the theme of nature covers a vast variety of aspects. Sometimes they are child-like in their simplicity and fairy-like in their intimacy but at time she looks deeper and finds that nature is a mysterious power which deals in destruction of man and leads him tragically to death. To her, Nature is a haunted-house. Emily Dickinson knew that she could not penetrate the unknowable or comprehend the deepest mysteries, but she insisted on asking questions. In her, we notice, the anguish of Shakespeare who wrote King Lear. She reveals an agonizing sense of ironic contrasts. She persistently asserts that intuition nor reason can solve the riddle of existence:

> But nature is a stranger yet;
> The ones that cite her most
> Have never passed her haunted house,
> Nor simplified her ghost[3]

Emily Dickinson wrote a number of love poems and the critics have tried to find out from these love poems the nature of her love-affair first with Newton, and then with Rev. Wadsworth. No doubt, she had a soft corner for Newton who died quite young and then she fell in love with Rev. Wadsworth, though this was all in vain because he was a married man and there was no hope of her being married to him. Thus naturally, crept in frustration in love, but much before her frustration in love, she had decided to dedicate herself to poetry and live an inner life. No doubt, her disappointment in love must have intensified and fortified that resolve.

Emily had transformed her experience of actual love into a spiritual experience. She was a woman of great integrity, purity, conscience and high sense of honour and her love-affair was conducted inwardly in her mind. That is why her poems on the theme of love are treated as mystical poems, and the lover is not an actual person, but some divine being, with whom she wants to establish an intimate relationship. Love seems to be closely associated with the spiritual aspect of her mystical attitude:

Unable are the loved to die
For love is immortality
Nay it is deity.[4]

Thus Emily Dickinson's love poems are much closer to her mystical concept of divine love than to the ordinary concept of earthly passion and marriage.

Given in marriage unto thee,
oh, thou celestial host !
Bride of the Father and the son
Bride of the Holy Ghost !
Other betrothal shall dissolve
Wedlock of will decay
Only the keeper of this seal
Conquers mortality[5]

Thus in most of her love poems, love has been lifted from the earthly to the idealistic stage, where everything seems to assume infinite proportions. These love poems bear no sign of complaints or mournings of lovers frustration in love or the pangs of separation. For Emily Dickinson, love is eternal, and suffers no change. It is perfect and everlasting, stead fast and fresh and ever the same. Her lover is not an actual person, but a "dim companion" living in the realm of her imagination, to whom she surrenders all her personality:

Doubt me, my dim companion !
Why, God would be content
Had I, a humble maiden
Whose farthest of degree
Was that she might
Dwell timidly with thee ![6]

All these love poems of Emily Dickinson are devoid of earthly passions. They breathe a spiritual atmosphere. Even when she sings of the agony of separation or frustration in love, such an experience is raised to the level of eternity. Living the life of a recluse these experience of love were enriched by her imagination and transformed into experience of the soul. No other nineteenth-century American poet, ever equalled the intensity of Miss Dickinson's love-lyrics. Her treatment of love is unique and marked throughout by originality.

Apart from Emily Dickinson's nature poems and love-poems, we find a bulk of poems, dealing with the theme of death and immortality. In fact, her poetic insight into nature of death may be regarded as one of her unique contribution to the nineteenth century American literature. Living an inner life, and probing the depths of her soul, she found that the problem of death and immortality is the biggest problem that the soul has to face. Her approach to these problems is unconventional, fresh and original and it gives us an insight into the subtle mind of Emily Dickinson who tried to form her judgements on these crucial problems on the basis of her spiritual intuition. Though some of her poems on Death embody her actual experience in real life, others convey the flashes of insight which she received in her inner soul.

Thus the themes of death and immortality provided Emily Dickinson as inexhaustible matrix for her poetic thoughts and imaginative experiences. They challenged her deeply introspective intellect and intrigued her sensibilities with a resistless fascination.

"Death profoundly and cruelly invited her. It was all when she tried to touch the smile" and dipped her 'fingers in the frost' that she took full possession of her genius.[7]

The poetry of Emily Dickinson shows a progression from sorrow and grief caused by the death of the people around her to the real nature of death that it is nothing but the door to immortality. Emily Dickinson's profound and original introspective insight enabled her to enrich her considerations of death with philosophic overtones. Few American poets have analysed and interpreted death with such variety and intensity.

Of course, Emily's poems on death, written earlier, present death as horror, a thing of fear and fright. But gradually she comprehends the true nature of death, that is harmless, and painless; and ultimately she comes to believe death as a kind visitor leading to immortality. Such matured outlook to death gives her the place of a mystic.

Here it would be worthwhile to compare Emily Dickinson with R.N. Tagore. Like Emily, Tagore also holds the view—

"on those days I never cared to know the meaning of songs thou singest to me. Only my voice took the tunes and my heart danced in their cadence.

Now, when the play time is over, what is this sudden sight that is come upon me ? The world with eyes bent upon thy feet stands in awe with all its silent tears.[8]

Emily Dickinson, who has witnessed death closely and minutely, is not at all puzzled at the sight of death rather welcomes it whole-heartedly. She prays to God "to tie the strings to her life as she is ready to take leave of the world, where she lived. This vision of Emily Dickinson corresponds to R.N. Tagore's vision of life hereafter, when he writes:

> "I have got my leave, Bid me,
> farewell, my brothers
> Here I give up all claims to my house
> I only ask for last kind words from you."[9]

Again in the next song (no. 94) of *Gitanjali* he sings:

"At this time of my parting, wish me good luck, my friends. The sky is flushed with dawn and my path lies beautiful.

Ask not what I have with me to take there. I start on my journey with empty hands and expectant heart ..."[10]

Thus, like Emily Dickinson, Tagore also seeks communion with God and death is the only means to achieve this divine end. Tagore sings in *Gitanjali*:

"And when my work shall be done in this world, O king of kings, alone and speechless shall I stand before thee face to face."[11]

The immediacy and the intensity of Emily's thought and passion found expression in concrete, sharply chiselled images that linger long in the imagination of all readers. It should be noted here that she anticipated the latter day Imagist School, founded by Ezra Pound.

Emily's quest for the colossal substance of Immortality continued with unabated fervour of spirit and imagination until the last day of her life. Like Browning, she too regarded, though with less certainty, the earthly existence as a palaestra for the education and refinement of the human soul. Browning's imagery of the potter and the clay on the wheel has been replaced in her poems with that of a Godhead, who, once envisaged as a stern Omnipotence, doling out punishment to the erring souls, becomes a benign and loving Father-figure, to whose benevolent—mentoring she surrenders herself in an attitude of wise passiveness:

How beautiful the dream
What plenty it would be
Had all my life but been mistake
Just rectified by Thee[12]

Emily Dickinson defies labels: Romantic, Transcendentalist Metaphysical, Meditative; she defies boundaries; she defies categories—religious, or lyric, or Nature poet. She is something of all these and more. But there is no doubt about her uniqueness and individuality. Like only the greatest she stands alone. Her place is among those whose gifts are too intrinsic for renown.

REFERENCES

1. Thomas H. Johnson (ed.), *The Complete Poems of Emily Dickinson.* (Delhi, Kalyani Publishers, 1960), Poem No. 252, p. 115.
2. *Ibid.*, Poem No. 1400, pp. 599-600.
3. *Ibid.*, Poem No. 809, p. 394.
4. *Ibid.*, Poem No. 817, p. 397.
5. *Ibid.*, Poem No. 275, pp. 125-126.
6. Richard B. Sewall (ed.), *Emily Dickinson: A Collection of Critical Essays* (Prentice-Hall Inc. U.S.A., 1963), p.15.
7. R.N. Tagore, *Gitanjali*, Poem No. 97 (Mcmillan & Co. Ltd., 1945), p. 89.
8. *Ibid.*, Song No. 93, p. 85.
9. *Ibid.*, p. 86.
10. *Ibid.*, Song No. 76, p. 71.
11. Johnson, *Complete Poems*, Poem No. 646, p. 321.
12. *Ibid.*, Poem No. 1393, p. 597.

TEXTUAL STUDY

Some more poems of Emily Dickinson of my choice, that justify her sound position as an American poetess are here for the readers. The text for this book, taken from 'The Complete Poems of Emily Dickinson' was compiled and edited by Thomas H. Johnson. The order of the poems is that of the Harvard (Variorum) edition.

My wheel is in the dark !
I cannot see a spoke
Yet know its dripping feet
Go round and round

My foot is on one Tide !
An unfrequented road -
Yet have all roads
A clearing at the end -

Some have resigned the Loom -
Some in the busy tomb
Find quaint employ -

Some with new - Stately feet -
Pass royal through the gate -
Flinging the problem back
At you and I

c - 1855 1914

(Poem No. 10, p. 10)

Poem No. 12

The norms are meeker than they were -
The nuts are getting brown -
The berry's cheek is plumper -
The Rose is out of town.

The Maple wears a gayer scarf -
The field a scarlet gown -
Lest I should be old fashioned
I'll put a trinket on.

Poem No. 25

She slept beneath a tree -
Remembered but by me -
I touched her Cradle mute -
She recognized the foot -
Put on her carmine suit
And see !

Poem No. 26

It's all I have to bring today -
This, and my heart beside -
This, and my heart, and all the fields -
And all the meadows wide -

Be sure you count - should I forget
Some one the sum could tell -
This, and my heart, and all the Beer
Which in the Clover dwell

Poem No. 27

Morns like these - We parted -
Noons live these - She rose -
Fluttering first - then firmer
To her fair repose.

Never did she lisp it -
It was not for me -

She - was mute from transport -
I - from agony -

Till - the evening nearing
One the curtains drew -
Quick ! A sharper rustling !
And this linnet flew !

Poem No. 29

If those I loved were lost
The Crier's voice would tell me -
If those I loved were found
The bells of Ghent would ring -

Did those I loved repose
The Daisy would impel me.
Philip - When bewildered
Box his riddle in !

Poem No. 38

By such and such an offering
To Mr So and So,
The web of life woven -
So martyrs albums show !

Poem No. 45

There's something quieter than sleep
Within this inner room !
It wears a sprig upon its breast -
And will not tell its name.

Some touch it, and some kiss it -
Some chafe its idle hand -
It has a simple gravity
I do not understand !

I would not weep if I were they -
How rude in one to sob !

Might scare the quiet fairy
Back to her native wood !

While simple - hearted neighbors
Chat of the 'Early dead' -
We - prove to periphrasis,
Remark that Birds have fled !

Poem No. 47

Heart ! We will forget him !
You and I - tonight !
You may forget the warmth he gave -
I will forget the light !

When you have done, Pray tell me
That I may straight begin !
Haste ! Last while you're lagging
I remember him !

Once more, my now bewildered Dove
Bestirs her puzzled wings
Once more her mistress, on the deep
Her troubled question flings -

Thrice to the floating casement
The Patriarch's bird returned,
Courage ! My brave Columba !
These may yet be Land !

Poem No. 49

I never lost as much but twice,
And that was in the Sad
Twice have I stood a beggar
Before the door of God !

Angels - twice descending
Reimbursed my store -
Burglar ! Barker - Father !
I am poor once more !

Poem No. 53

Taken from mean - thus morning -
Carried by men today -
Met by the Gods with banners -
Who marshaled her away -

One little maid - from playmates
One little mind from school -
There must be guests in Eden -
All the rooms are full -

Far - as the East from Even -
Dim - as the border star -
Courtiers quaint, in kingdoms
Our departed are.

Poem No. 56

If I should cease to bring a Rose
Upon a festal day,
'T will be because beyond the Rose
I have been called away -

If I should cease to take the names
My buds commemorate -
'T' will be because Death's finger
Claps my murmuring lip !

Poem No. 61

Papa above !
Regard a Mouse
O' erpowered by the Cat !
Reserve within they Kingdom
A 'Mansion' for the Rat !

Snug in Seraphic Cupboards
To nibble all the day,
While unsuspecting cycles
Wheel solemnly away !

Poem No. 92

My friend must be a Bird -
Because it flies !
Mortal, my friend must be,
Because it dies !
Barbs has it, like a Bee !
An, curious friend !
Thou puzzlest me !

Poem No. 101

Will there really be a 'Morning' ?
Is there such a thing as 'Day' ?
Could I see it from the mountains
If I were as tall as they ?

Has it feet like Water lilies ?
Has it feathers like a Bird ?
Is it brought from famous countries
Of which I have never heard ?

Oh some Scholar ! Oh some Sailor !
Oh some Wise Man from the skies !
Please to tell a little Pilgrim
Where the place called 'Morning' lies !

Poem No. 274

It's easy to invest a life -
God does it - every Day -
Creation - but the Gambol
Of His Authority -

It's easy to efface it -
The thrifty Deity
Could scarce afford eternity
To Spontaneity

The Perished Patterns murmur -
But His Perturbless Plan

Proceed - inserting Here - a Sun -
There - leaving out a Man -

Poem No. 786

Severer Service of myself
I - hastened to demand
To fill the awful Vacuum
Your life had left behind -

I worried Nature with my Wheels
When Hers had ceased to run -
When she had put away Her Work.
My own had just begun.

I strove to Weary Brain and Bone -
To harass to fatigue
The glittering Retinue of nerves -
Vitality to Clog

To some dull comfort those obtain
Who put a Head away
They knew the Hair to -
And forget the color of the Day -

Affliction would not be appeased -
The Darkness braced as firm
As all my Stratagem had been
The Midnight to confirm -

No Drug for Consciousness - can be -
Alternative to die
Is Nature's only Pharmacy
For Being's Malady -

SOME MORE POEMS BY MISS DICKINSON

Not In Vain

If I can stop one heart from breaking,
I shall not live in vain;
If I can ease one life the aching,
Or cool one pain,
Or help one fainting robin
Unto his nest again,
I shall not live in vain.

A word is dead

A word is dead
When it is said,
Some say.

I say it just
Begins to live
That day.

The Forgotten Grave

After a hundred years
Nobody knows the place,—
Agony that enacted there,
Motionless as peace.

Weeds triumphant ranged,
Strangers strolled and spelled
At the lone orthography
Of the elder dead.

Winds of summer fields
Recollect the way,—
Instinct picking up the key
Dropped by memory.

I have Not Told My Garden Yet

I have not told my garden yet,
Lest that should conquer me;
I have not quite the strength now
To break it to the bee.

I will not name it in the street,
For shops would stare, that I,
So shy, so very ignorant,
Should have the face to die.

The hillsides must not know it,
Where I have rambled so,
Nor tell the loving forests
The day that I shall go,

Nor lisp it at the table,
Nor heedless by the way
Hint that within the riddle
One will walk to-day!

This Is My Letter To The World

This is my letter to the world,
That never wrote to me,—
The simple news that Nature told,
With tender majesty.
Her message is committed
To hands I cannot see;
For love of her, sweet countrymen,
Judge terderly of me!

Love is anterior to life

Love is anterior to life,
Posterior to death,
Initial of creation, and
The exponent of breath.

We never know how high we are

We never know how high we are
Till we are called to rise;
And then, if we are true to plan,
Our statures touch the skies.

The heroism we recite
Would be a daily thing,
Did not ourselves the cubits warp
For fear to be king.

How happy is the little stone

How happy is the little stone
That rambles in the road alone,
And doesn't care about careers,
And exigencies never fears;
Whose coat of elemental brown
A passing universe put on;
And independent as the sun,
Associates or glows alone,
Fulfilling absolute decree
In casual simplicity.

I felt a clearing in my mind

I felt a clearing in my mind
As if my brain had split;
I tried to match it, seam by seam,
But could not make them fit.

The thought behind I strove to join
Unto the thought before,

But sequence ravelled out of reach
Like balls upon the floor.

Look Back On Time with Kindly Eyes

Look back on time with kindly eyes,
He doubtless did his best;
How softly sinks his trembling sun
In human nature's west!

Farewell

Tie the strings to my life, my Lord,
Then I am ready to go!
Just a look at the horses—
Rapid! That will do!

Put me in on the firmest side,
So I shall never fall;
For we must ride to the Judgement,
And it's partly down hill.
But never I mind the bridges,
And never I mind the sea;
Held fast in everlasting race
By my own choice and thee.

Good-bye to the life I used to live,
And the world I used to know;
And kiss the hills for me, just once;
Now I am ready to go!

My Nosegays Are For Captives

My nosegays are for captives;
Dim, long-expectant eyes,
Fingers denied the plucking,
Patient till paradise.

To such, if they should whisper
Of morning and the moor,

They bear no other errand,
And I, no other prayer.

Because I could not stop for Death

Because I could not stop for Death—
He kindly stopped for me—
The Carriage held but just Ourselves—
and Immortality.

We slowly drove—He knew no haste
And I had put away
My labor and my leisure too,
For His Civility—

We passed the School, where Children stro
At Recess—in the Ring—
We passed the Fields of Gazing Grain—
We passed the Setting Sun—

Or rather—He passed Us—
The Dews drew quivering and chill—
For only Gossamer, my Gown—
My Tippet—only Tulle—

We paused before a House that seemed
A Swelling of the Ground—
The Roof was scarcely visible—
The Cornice—in the Ground—

Since then— 'Tis Centuries—and yet
Feels shorter than the Day
I first surmised the Horses Heads
Were toward Eternity—

BIBLIOGRAPHY

Ackmann, Martha. *The Matrilineage of Emily Dickinson,* Diss. University of Massachusetts, 1988.

Agrawal, Abha. *Emily Dickinson, Search for Self*. New Delhi: Young Asia Publications, 1977.

Benfy, Christopher. *Emily Dickinson: Lives of a Poet*. New York: Braziller, 1986.

Bennett, Paula. *Emily Dickinson: Woman Poet*, Iowa City: University of Iowa Press, 1990.

Bianchi, Martha Gilbert Dickinson. *Emily Dickinson Face to Face: Unpublished Letters with Notes and Reminiscences by Her Niece*. Boston: Houghton Mifflin, 1932.

Bloom, Harold (ed). *Emily Dickinson: Modern Critical Views*. New York: Chelsea House, 1985.

Buckingham, Wills J. *Emily Dickinson, an Annotated Bibliography: Writings, Scholarship, Criticism, and Ana, 1850—1968*. Bloomington, IN: Indiana University Press, 1970.

Burr, Zofia A. *Of Women, Poetry, and Power: Strategies of Address in Dickinson, Miles, Brooks, Lorde, and Angelou*. Chicago: University of Illinois Press, 2002.

Capps, Jack L. *Emily Dickinson's Reading, 1836—1886*. Cambridge, MA: Harvard University Press, 1966.

Carton, Evan. *The Rhetoric of American Romance: Dialectic and Identity in Emerson, Dickinson, Poe and Hawthorne*. Baltimore: Johns Hopkins University Press, 1985.

Chesnokova, Anna. *Emily Dickinson in Ukrainian Literary Studies*, Emily Dickinson International Society Bulletin. Vol. 13, No. 1 (May/June, 2001).

Conrad, Angela. *The Wayward Nun of Amherst: Emily Dickinson in the Medieval Women's Visionary Tradition.* New York: Garland Publishing, 2000.

Crumbley, Paul. *Inflections of the Pen: Dash and Voice in Emily Dickinson.* Lexington: University Press of Kentucky, 1997.

Danly, Susan. *Language as Object: Emily Dickinson and Contemporary Art.* Amherest: University of Massachusetts Press, 1997.

Diehl, Joanne Feit. *Dickinson and the Romantic Imagination.* Princeton: Princeton University Press, 1981.

—. *Women Poets and the American Sublime.* Bloomington: Indiana University Press, 1990.

Duchac, Joseph. *The Poems of Emily Dickinson: An Annotated Guide to Commentary.* Boston: G.K. Hall, 1979.

Erkkila, Betsy. *The Wicked Sisters: Women Poets, Literary History, and Discord.* New York: Oxford University Press, 1992.

—. *The Passion of Emily Dickinson.* Cambridge, MA: Harvard University Press, 1992.

Farr, Judith with Louise Carter. *The Gardens of Emily Dickinson.* Cambridge: Harvard University Press, 2004.

Ford, Thomas W. *Heaven Beguiles the Tired: Death in the Poetry of Emily Dickinson.* Tuscaloosa: University of Alabama Press, 1966.

Freeman, Margaret H. Gudrun Grabher, and Roland Hogenbuchle, (eds.). *There's a certain Slant of light: Swedish, Finnish, Chinese, Japanese, Yiddish.* The Emily Dickinson Journal 6, 2 (1997): 38-72.

Fuss, Diana. *The Sense of an Interior: Four Rooms and the Writers That Shaped Them.* New York: Routledge, 2004.

Gelpi, Albert J. *Emily Dickinson: The Mind of the Poet.* Cambridge: Harvard University Press, 1965.

Gilbert, Sandra M. and Susan Gubar. *The Madwoman in the Attic: The Woman Writer and the Nineteenth-Century Literary Imagination.* New Haven: Yale University Press, 1979.

Gould, Jean, Illus. by Ursula Koening. Miss Emily. Boston: Houghton Mifflin Co., 1946.

Higgins, David. *Portrait of Emily Dickinson: The Poet and Her Prose.* New Brunswick, NJ: Rutgers University Press, 1967.

Howe, Susan. *My Emily Dickinson.* Berkeley, CA: North Atlantic Books, 1985.

Hunt, Helen. *Faith and Feminism: A Holy Alliance.* New York: Simon & Schuster, 2004.

Johnson, Thomas H. *Emily Dickinson: An Interpretive Biography.* Cambridge: Harvard University Press, Belknap Press, 1955.

Kirkby, Joan. *Emily Dickinson. Women Writers Series.* London: Macmillan, 1991.

Knapp, Bettina L. *Emily Dickinson.* New York: Continuum, 1989.

Lebo, Lori. *Autobiographic Self-Construction in the Letters of Emily Dickinson*, University of Wollongong, Australia, 1999.

Leder, Sharen and Andrea Abbott. *The Language of Exclusion: The Poetry of Emily Dickinson and Christina Rossetti.* Westport, CT: Greenwood Press, 1987.

Longsworth, Polly. *The World of Emily Dickinson.* New York: Norton, 1990.

Loving, Jerome. *Emily Dickinson: The Poet on the Second Story.* Cambridge: Cambridge University Press, 1986.

McDowell, Marta. *Emily Dickinson's Gardens: Discovering the Flowers That Inspired Her Poetry.* New York: McGraw-Hill, 2004.

Miller, Cristanne. *Emily Dickinson: A Poet's Grammar.* Cambridge, MA: Harvard University Press, 1987.

Miller, Ruth. *The Poetry of Emily Dickinson*. Middletown, CT: Wesleyan University Press, 1968.

Olney, James. *The Languages of Poetry: Walt Whitman, Emily Dickinson, Gerard Manley Hopkins*. Athens, GA: University of Georgia Press, 1993.

Pollitt, Josephine. *Emily Dickinson: The Human Background of Her Poetry*. New York: Harper, 1930.

Pritchard, William H. *Talking Back to Emily Dickinson and Other Essays*. Amherst, MA: University Press, 1998.

Rich, Adrienne. *Vesuvius at Home: The Power of Emily Dickinson*. On Lies, Secrets, and Silence: Selected Prose 1966-1978. 1976. New York: Norton, 1979. 157-83.

Rupp, Richard H. *Critics on Emily Dickinson*. Miami, FL: University of Miami Press, 1972.

Stonum, Gary Lee. *The Dickinson Sublime*. Madison, WI: University of Wisconsin Press, 1990.

Taggard, Genevieve. *The Life and Mind of Emily Dickinson*. New York: A.A. Knopf, 1930.

Thackrey, Donard E. *Emily Dickinson's Approach to Poetry*. Lincoln: University of Nebraska, 1954.

Thota, Anand Rao. *Foreword by Satyanarain Singh. Emily Dickinson: The Metaphysical Tradition*. Atlantic Highlands, NJ: Humanities, 1982.

Uno, Hiroko. *Emily Dickinson Visits Boston*. Kyoto, Japan: Yamaguchi Publishing House, 1990.

Untermeyer, Louis, (ed.). *Emily Dickinson, 1830—1886*. New York: Simon & Schuster, 1927.

Ward, Bruce. *The Gift of Screws: The Poetic Strategies of Emily Dickinson*. Troy, NY: Whitson Publishing, 1994.

Weisbuch, Robert. *Emily Dickinson's Poetry*. Chicago: The University of Chicago Press, 1975.

Wells, Henry Willis. *Introduction to Emily Dickinson*. Chicago: Hendricks House, 1947.

Whicher, George Frisbie. *This Was a Poet: A Critical Biography of Emily Dickinson.* New York: Charles Scribner's Sons, 1938.

Wolosky, Shira. *Emily Dickinson: A Voice of War.* New Haven, CT: Yale University Press, 1984.

Wylder, Edith. *The Last Face: Emily Dickinson's Manuscripts.* Albuquerque, NM: University of New Mexico Press, 1971.